Shepherd-sheepdog mix

HOW TO SPEAK DoG

A GUIDE TO DECODING DOG LANGUAGE

by Aline Alexander Newman
& Gary Weitzman, D.V.M.

President & CEO of the
San Diego Humane Society

NATIONAL GEOGRAPHIC

WASHINGTON, D.C.

CoNTENTS

French
bulldog

MEET DR. GARY

VETERINARIAN AND DOG EXPERT

MAYBE YOU ALREADY have a dog. Maybe you're hoping to get one. A dog can be your BFF and lovable companion for many years. But to get the most out of your relationship, you need to communicate. Dogs already understand some human language. So isn't it time you learned to speak "dog"?

My name is Dr. Gary Weitzman, and I'm going to be your guide throughout this book. I have two awesome dogs, Jake and Betty, who are my perfect pals. For more than 20 years, I've been working as a veterinarian and helping organizations rescue

animals. I'm currently the president of the San Diego Humane Society in California, U.S.A., and before that I ran the Washington Animal Rescue League, a big animal shelter in Washington, D.C. Both of these groups rescue and take care of thousands of dogs from all over the country every year. Communicating with the dogs we rescue is a very important aspect of taking care of them. Once we are able to understand their behaviour and what they're trying to tell us, we're better able to help them recover and find loving adoptive families.

Throughout this book, I'll tell you different tips that I use to communicate with dogs so that you can use the same skills to talk to your own furry friends. My hope is that by the end of the book, you and your dog understand one another so well you'll become even better pals!

Just remember, like humans, every dog is an individual with its own unique set of needs. People use many techniques to train dogs, but most dog

Jack Russell terrier

trainers, educators, and behaviour professionals agree that you must first understand and be able to communicate with them. Whether it's reading their body language, listening to the sounds they make, or simply knowing why they like or dislike certain foods, once you are able to better understand each other, the bond between you and your dog will be so much stronger.

Scientists recently discovered that dogs recognize their owner's face. What's more, they read our expressions. "Uh-oh. She's feeling grumpy," your dog might decide. "Guess I'll stay out of her hair." Or, "Look at that smile! Maybe we'll go to the park!" Scientists also know that dogs share human emotions. They feel happy, sad, excited, and scared. But to interpret dog feelings, we have to look closely. Dogs talk to us with their entire body, including eyes, ears, mouth, tail, posture, and voice. All of these signals have multiple meanings. Only by putting them together can we figure out what a dog is saying.

So keep reading. Besides your own, "Dog Speak" may be the most important language you ever learn.

FOR YOUR SAFETY

While National Geographic has worked to make sure the following training tips, scenarios, and interpretations of dog behaviour come from the most accurate and up-to-date sources, you should know that dogs, like all animals, can be unpredictable.

No matter how careful you are, no matter how many rules you follow, things can go wrong. Also, much of the advice and guidance in this book requires close observation of dogs; there may be nuances of behaviour that the observer can miss. So even though this book is packed with advice from the experts, there is no guarantee that such advice will work in any specific situation. Always be cautious with dogs who are strangers to you and careful with dogs with whom you are familiar.

All content and information published in this book is provided to the reader "as is" and without any guarantees. The situations and activities described carry inherent risks and hazards. The reader must evaluate and accept all risks associated with the use of the information provided in this book, including those risks associated with reliance on the accuracy, thoroughness, utility, or appropriateness of the information for any particular situation. The authors and publisher specifically disclaim all responsibility for any liability, loss, or risk, personal or otherwise, which is incurred as a consequence of the application of any of the contents in this book.

WHAT IS A DOG?

TAIL: You could say dogs wear their heart on their tail. A fast-wagging tail is like a furry smiley face. A droopy tail is a frown.

Malinois

PAWS: Dogs walk on their toes. Some breeds, including Newfoundlands and Chesapeake Bay retrievers, have webbed feet like a duck.

COAT: The colour, length, texture, and thickness of a dog's coat varies by breed. Light-coloured dogs can sunburn, especially their ears and noses.

MUZZLE: A wrinkled muzzle may mean a dog is relaxed, while a pulled-back muzzle may mean he's tense and looking for a fight (or to avoid one!). Some "snub-nosed" dogs, such as pugs, aren't really able to do much with the little nose they've got, but they sure work to get their point across!

EARS: Strong facial muscles connected to each ear let dogs rotate, tilt, raise, and lower one ear at a time.

EYES: Dogs have three eyelids—an upper, a lower, and a third in the inside corner of their eye. This third eyelid wipes the eyeball clear of debris.

NOSE: Sticky fluid from glands inside a dog's nose keeps the tip wet. This fluid catches scent molecules and helps detect odours.

TEETH: Puppies lose their baby teeth when they reach four months of age. That's when their permanent teeth start to grow in.

TONGUE: Like humans, dogs taste with their tongue. They only have 1,700 taste buds, compared to the 9,000 we humans have, but they have some special taste buds just for tasting water and fat.

DoG FAMILY BARKFEST

Five million years ago, a fox-sized creature called Leptocyon roamed Earth. Leptocyon's descendants split into two groups—dogs and foxes. The dog family includes the "father" of the domestic dog—the wolf—and several "uncles". Here's how they communicate:

JACKAL
Loudest "Talker"

Jackals mate for life, and the noisy couples yap and scream up a storm. But each family has its own secret lingo, which prevents outsiders from figuring out what they're saying.

AFRICAN WILD DOG
Weirdest Voice

Wild dogs sound nothing like they look. Ferocious hunters, they twitter and chirp like birds. And if one gets lost, it calls for help by making a noise like a ringing bell.

LEPTOCYON

About the only thing scientists know about this prehistoric creature is that it didn't live by eating meat alone. It had small teeth suited to chomping up berries and fruits as well as rodents and rabbits. This ability to eat a varied diet came in very handy and was passed on to wolves.

FOX (VULPINI)
Biggest Vocab

Foxes bark, whimper, pant, squeak, yap, and more. As one scientist wrote, "Foxes do everything, except howl and meow."

TRUE DOGS

FOX

WOLF
Champion Howler

Wolves communicate using body language, scent, and sound. They bark, whine, whimper, and growl. But most often they howl. Howling is a ghostly sound similar to the wind blowing through the trees—and it can be heard up to 10 miles away! Wolves do it to find each other and to warn off intruders.

DINGO
Canine Copycat

Wild dingoes don't bark. They howl like wolves and for the same reasons. But captive dingoes can sometimes learn to bark by listening to domestic dogs.

COYOTE
Biggest Name-dropper

Every coyote's voice sounds different. These night-time songsters call out their age, size, gender, and mood with every howl.

DOMESTIC DOG
Best Listener

Domestic dogs not only "talk", they listen. They are the only pups born caring what we humans have to say. No wonder we love 'em.

Dalmatian mixed breed

Test your doggie knowledge! Can you match each dog's posture to the correct emotion? Fill in each box with the correct letter. (Check your answers below.)

1. **CURIOUS** "Whuzzup?"

2. **SUBMISSIVE** "Just tell me what you want. You're the boss!"

3. **LONELY** "I'm all alone. Where did everybody go?"

4. **PLAYFUL** "Throw me the ball!"

5. **AFRAID** "I'll do anything you want. Please don't hurt me."

6. **AGGRESSIVE** "Back off, now— before somebody gets hurt!"

A Belgian shepherd

D Border collie

B German short-haired pointer

E Border collie

C Wire fox terrier

F Dachshund

Golden retriever.

BoDY TALK

DOGS ARE LIKE ACTORS. Turn on the television, but turn off the volume. Watch in silence for a few minutes. Study the actors, and you can probably tell how each one is feeling. Perhaps a child is excited. A woman might show surprise, or a man could act angry.

Because of the way their voice boxes are built, dogs can't make as many sounds as people can. Most of the time, they're quiet. Watch a group of dogs playing together at a dog park. They don't know each other, yet within a few minutes of meeting, they'll start playing some doggie game. As they wrestle and chase, it's obvious they are "talking". But, instead of words, they're using body language. You can learn to read their body language, too!

Look at how a dog is holding her body. Is she all loose and wiggly? Then she's probably happy and friendly. But beware a nervous dog. His body will usually be stiff and tight. Also realize that like humans, any dog can "say" one thing and mean another. But learning to speak dog is fun, and doing so will go a long way toward helping you get closer to your hound.

WHAT
ARE YOU
WAITING FOR?
LET'S MOVE IT!
MOVE IT!

DR. GARY'S VET TIPS

SOME PEOPLE control their dog by using a choke collar made of metal chain. When their dog disobeys, they jerk the chain. I think choke collars should be thrown into the bin. Dogs are smart. There's no need to communicate with them through pain. I recommend using what's called a "sensation" harness. It steers a dog from the chest, not the neck, and discourages him from pulling.

Border terrier

TUGGING ON the LEAD

Do you walk your dog, or does he walk you? If Fluffy strains so hard against the lead that you have to run, experts say two things are happening.

First, in a dog's world, one of you must lead. The other must follow. Show Fluffy you're the leader by always staying in front. Second, if your dog is so strong you can't hold him back, give him more exercise. Dogs really need four basic things: exercise, mental stimulation, rewards, and affection. After all, dogs were bred to work. They once herded cattle, hunted ducks, and pulled carts—among dozens of other tasks. Now, most are unemployed couch-cuddlers!

There are many ways to teach proper walking behaviour. One way is to work off your dog's excess energy by playing hard with him. Toss a Frisbee for him to catch, play fetch with a tennis ball, or train him to jump hurdles. Then, when you go for walks, shorten the lead and walk faster. With luck, he'll eventually fall into step just behind your left foot. That's called "heeling" or "walking on a loose lead". It puts you in control and makes dog walking more fun—for both you and your canine.

Joe Orsino, of Pennsylvania, U.S.A., holds the Guinness World Record for the most dogs walked by one person at the same time—35.

Jack Russell terrier

Golden retriever

the FULL-BODY SHAKE

It happens all the time in sports. A batter gets hit with the ball or two football players collide. Their coach lets them moan and hop around for a minute or two, then . . . "Shake it off!" the coach says. The player shakes whatever hurts (and often his head), and the game continues. Dogs do the same thing, especially after a swim. Your dripping wet pooch climbs out of the water and comes straight to you. You scramble to escape, but seconds later Lady looks blow-dried and fluffy, while you're the one soaked.

But believe it or not, dogs also shake when their fur is bone-dry.

Maybe you've just returned home. "Yippee!" thinks your pooch, who wiggles and jumps, barking excitedly, while you shower him with hugs and kisses. It's a great reunion, but all that loving can be too much. So when you walk away, your hyped-up dog might shake all over.

Dogs also may do the dry dog shake after a rough play session, a meet-up with a doggie friend, or any episode that feels super-intense. Why? Like the injured athlete, your dog is trying to distract himself and calm down. It usually works.

A wet dog can shake himself almost completely dry in less than one second!

Black and white havanese

PAW ON YOUR KNEE

 It happens a lot. A dog sits and puts his paw on your knee. "How sweet," you think. And that could be, especially if he's learned that this is a way into your heart. But that may be the farthest thought from Buster's mind. He actually may be trying to get you to hand him that biscuit you're eating!

Every dog pack has a leader. Good leaders get to the top by earning the respect of the dogs under them. They get that respect by being smart and strong and by showing a lot of attitude. Some dogs, big breeds especially, can get carried away. They show this same attitude with their owners. A large mutt might try to make himself "king" by standing on his hind legs and putting his paws on your shoulders. Or—you guessed it— he might put his paw on your knee.

That isn't always the case. If your dog puts his paw on your knee and wiggles it under your hand, he doesn't have "king" on his mind. He really is just being sweet. So do as he asks and give him a pat.

Willow the English terrier mix can "read". She sits when she sees the words "sit up" and raises her paw when she sees the word "wave"!

Golden doodle

21

LYING BELLY-UP

Rub a dub, dub. Time for a belly rub. That's what it looks like a dog is saying when she rolls onto her back with her front legs bent and her belly exposed. When you start rubbing, sometimes one hind leg will kick, and she will look as contented as can be. The kicking leg is just a reflex— kind of like what happens when the doctor taps your knee with a rubber hammer. But the real meaning of this dog's position is submission and trust. She's saying that you're in charge, and she's okay with that.

The message is the same if she bares her belly to another dog. Most dogs won't hurt a dog that is signalling submission. They'll simply sniff her rear end and maybe stand over her, showing the world that they are "top dog".

But baring the belly always puts a dog at risk. There's no way she can defend herself if she meets with a bully. Good thing most dogs play by the rules.

Stroking a dog is healthy for people. It slows our pulse and lowers our blood pressure.

I WON'T BE A PROBLEM, BOSS. I'LL DO ANYTHING YOU WANT.

Dachshund

Bernese mountain dog

WIGGLES AWAY FROM YOU

Snuggle. Cuddle. Who doesn't like to be hugged? Dogs! That's who. When you hug Rocky, you're restricting him. It's like tying him on a short rope, only worse. With your arms around him, a dog can't move his legs or his head. He might not even be able to move his tail. As a result, he has also lost most of his ways to communicate. Hugging might feel as scary to a dog as it would to you if a bigger kid sat on your chest and refused to get off.

What's a dog to do? A dog being hugged by his beloved owner might tolerate feeling so trapped. He might even enjoy it because he trusts his person. But if a stranger is doing the hugging, a dog could panic—especially if the stranger is leaning over him. In dog speak, that means the human is trying to become dominant. Is it any wonder that the dog feels anxious and wiggles and squirms to get away? He may even snap or threaten to bite.

A snug-fitting jacket called the "Thundershirt" applies **gentle, constant pressure that** helps calm **dogs during** thunderstorms or when the **vacuum is running.**

DR. GARY'S VET TIPS

MANY DOGS are okay with hugging, once they get used to it. But, in general, dogs are not comfortable being so restricted, and it makes them uneasy. If you're in the mood for a furry snuggle, invite your hound to sit or lie down right next to you. Some dogs, even big dogs that look ridiculous doing it, love sitting on their owner's lap!

FREEZING IN PLACE

Something's wrong—that's for sure. Whenever a dog freezes in place, he's letting you know he's afraid. A frightened dog has four choices: he can fight; he can play nice, hoping to defuse the situation; he can run; or he can freeze. Any dog that stops moving and suddenly becomes as still as a statue is hoping that if he does nothing, his enemy will calm down and go away. This often works with other dogs.

That's because our pooches, as cousins of wolves, are naturally attracted to movement. Just think how a dog will chase a bicycle being pedalled down the street, but ignore a bike lying in the grass.

Humans, however, are another story. We don't automatically lose interest just because something stops moving. So this is one of those times when it's really important to think like a dog. If you see a loose dog approaching, and he freezes in place—you should stop. Stand perfectly still. Let the dog make the first move. That's the best way to make sure nobody gets hurt.

A sharp-eyed **greyhound** can recognize its owner from a **mile** away if he's waving his arms.

Jack Russell terrier

the PLAY-BOW

Great Danes do it, and so do Chihuahuas. All dogs do it, from the Americas to Zambia, and everywhere else around the world. It's called the play-bow, and it means your dog is ready for fun! One dog will approach another with a relaxed look on her face. She'll crouch down with her "elbows" almost touching the ground, her tail waving madly, and her rump in the air. After holding this pose for a few seconds, she'll take off running, checking over her shoulder to make sure the other dog is following.

If her new playmate comes bounding after her, the two dogs will race and chase, weaving between trees and jumping over obstacles. First one dog will take the lead. Then the other might take a turn. If either dog missteps or bangs into the other too hard, it'll do a quick play-bow mid-chase to make amends.

Dogs are born to run and play, and they will play alone. But, like you, they'd rather play with a friend. So if your dog does a play-bow to you, go ahead and be a sport.

Let the games begin!

COME ON! I DARE YOU. CATCH ME IF YOU CAN.

Augie, a golden retriever from Texas, U.S.A., holds the **world record** for gathering and holding the most tennis balls in his mouth—**five!**

DR. GARY'S VET TIPS

SUPPOSE YOUR dog ignores her toys and never fetches a thrown stick. Don't worry about it. Like people, all dogs have individual personalities. Some bark, eat, or play more than others. But if your normally playful pooch suddenly starts lying down instead of chasing a bouncing ball, take notice. She may be scared, anxious, tired, or sick. Any repeated behaviour that is new or different is a warning sign to visit your vet.

Border collie

Chihuahua

PLEASED TO MEET YOU, SIR. YOUR WISH IS MY COMMAND.

ONE PAW RAISED

It looks so simple. You're meeting a strange dog for the first time, and he sits and raises one paw. Should you grab it and shake? No. That's what many people do, but it's a violation of doggie etiquette. A dog doing this isn't offering his paw for someone to hold. He's feeling nervous and unsure and raising his foot as a sign of submission.

Dogs walk on their paws. They don't carry things in them or use them like hands. And they certainly don't use them to greet others. Dogs will "shake hands" on command, if someone has taught them to. But they don't do it naturally.

A dog lifting a paw is like a commoner bowing before a king. Many humans might eventually rebel, but dogs actually like it this way. The underdogs feel safe knowing someone else is in charge, and the top dog doesn't need to fight to re-establish his rank. So don't touch. Just acknowledge the gesture with a kind word or two. The dog will love you for it.

When German countess Carlotta Liebenstein died, she left £62 million to Gunther III, her beloved German shepherd.

German short-haired pointer

POINTING

Dogs understand gestures. This too, experts say, probably comes from their wolf ancestors. When plotting to bring down a deer, the lead wolf assigns each member of his pack a battle position. But wolves can't talk or read. So how do they understand their assignment?

In the pack, the lead wolf will first look at another. Then he turns his head, with its pointed muzzle, in the exact direction he wants the other wolf to go. The leader does this again and again, until all the wolves are where he wants them. Then, bang! It's like an action movie. Two wolves spring forward together. The deer runs, but it's trapped. Wolves block every path of escape.

Like wolves, dogs point by turning their heads and bodies. Duck hunters use specially bred dogs, such as pointers and setters, to help them find birds. But regular mutts can point, too. You just have to look closely.

Look closely the next time Bentley barks at something. See how he's standing and which direction his head is facing. He might be trying to tell you something.

Dogs not only point themselves. They also understand when humans do it and will go to wherever their person directs them.

BRISTLING

Having a bad hair day? To you, that means that your hair looks a mess. To a dog, it's when she gets her hackles up. Hackles are the hairs on a dog's back and shoulders that act like goose bumps on your skin. A dog that is angry or afraid may deliberately raise them, because having her hair stand on end makes her look bigger and scarier.

But some experts don't think dogs have any control over their hair at all. Like goose bumps, hackles might just happen all by themselves. Either way, a dog with its hackles up is ready to fight.

This is easy to see on a short-haired canine. The hair stands up like the bristles on a hairbrush. Not so for an Old English sheepdog or any other long-haired canine. In that case, you should look for other signs. You need to do that anyway, because that's the best way to judge a dog's mood.

Sometimes the bristling goes all the way from a dog's neck to the tip of her tail. Stay on the safe side. Don't run. Just back away slowly, but do get out of there!

The komondor, a Turkish **guard dog,** is covered in twisted cords of long, white hair that look like the strings on a cotton floor **mop.**

Rhodesian ridgebacks

WHAT SHOULD you do if two dogs start to fight? Stay back! Don't get near them. If either dog is on a lead, pull at the lead until the dogs are separated. But don't pick up a dog that's been in a fight. That only makes it worse. An aggressive dog might attack you.

WHAT IS THIS DoG SAYING?

The Scenario

Dr. Gary was walking his two dogs, Betty and Jake, down the street in Washington, D.C. Everything was calm. Betty was eating grass on the edge of a lawn, and Jake was sniffing the base of a tree. All of a sudden, a jogger ran by with her yellow Lab. But she didn't just run by at a safe distance—she ran right between Betty and Jake.

Betty didn't even notice. But Jake did. He suddenly got pushy—barking, pulling at the lead, and going berserk.

You Be the Expert

So what happened? What was Jake saying? What was Betty saying?

Jake was surprised and caught off guard when the Lab ran close to him. Jake actually responded normally for his personality—he "spoke" his mind. Humans sometimes feel caught off guard when scared or startled, too. We may yell, try to run away, or even get a little mad. Canine reactions are not so different from ours!

So why did Jake react the way he did while Betty just acted like everything was normal?

When a dog "reacts" to another, there could be lots of happy wagging (that's what Betty would do), or freezing, stiffening up, barking, and lunging. Jake acts up when he sees another dog because he may feel threatened. Sometimes dog-reactive hounds can

be outright aggressive, which can be very dangerous. The solution is to learn doggie body talk.

Listening to Your Dog

If you're walking your dog and see another, always stop before approaching. Let the dogs tell you with their body language if they want to meet. Look at their eyes, tails, and shoulders. Is the other dog staring directly at yours? In dog speak, that's rude! Then, look at its tail. A broad, happy tail wag is friendly. A tucked tail or one held high and wagging stiffly just at the tip is not. Is the dog "frozen" in place with stiff shoulders? If any of these things are happening, definitely don't approach. Always ask the other owner if it's OK for your dogs to meet. Always check out the body language of other dogs yourself to make sure you feel it's safe.

What if your dog doesn't calm down? A good trainer can offer advice and help bring out the best in dog-reactive pooches. In the end, they might not love other dogs, but they will be safer around their canine cousins.

The bottom line is to know your dog, and remember that you don't always know other people's dogs. And even when you do, you still need to be careful.

Golden Labrador retriever and Jack Russell terrier

RED ROVER, RED ROVER, SEND MY DOG OVER!

Teaching your dog to "come"

 1 Start with your pooch a short distance away on-lead. Hold his favourite toy or small pieces of a yummy treat in one hand and his lead in the other.

 2 Say your dog's name and the command word "come" in a happy and excited voice so your dog will be excited to come to you. Get down and pat the floor or your thigh to help him get the right idea.

 3 When Rover comes running, say what a good job he did and give him his tasty reward! He'll associate the behaviour with positive feelings—good incentive to do it again next time.

 4 Practise five minutes a day, gradually increasing the space between you and your canine companion until he's coming your way from a good distance.

 5 What if Rover refuses to come over? Make sure to be patient and keep working with your pooch. Stop the activity and pick it up again another time if you or your dog gets frustrated or tired.

English bulldog

Pug

REaD MY FACE

DOGS DIDN'T START out looking so different from each other. In the beginning, they all looked like wolves. That's because thousands of years ago, early humans started domesticating (taming) grey wolves to serve as watchdogs and help them hunt. Later, humans began acting as matchmakers. They paired off the wolves to get puppies that were even better watchdogs and hunters. Over time, some wolves evolved into dogs, our first animal friends.

But humans kept tinkering. Dogs now have perked or floppy ears. They have round-, oval-, almond-, or diamond-shaped eyes. People began mixing and matching to get big dogs and little dogs, dogs to herd sheep and dogs to hunt badgers.

Today, almost 400 breeds of dogs exist, in all different colours, shapes, and sizes. But not all changes have been good. Flat-faced dogs, like pugs and Pekingese, sometimes have trouble breathing. And the puli has so much long, shaggy hair that to see the look on his face, you'd have to buy him a hair band.

All dogs, no matter what shape or size, speak with their faces. And no matter what those look like, you, too, can learn to read their many expressions.

DR. GARY'S VET TIPS

MOST PEOPLE FOOD is fine for dogs, unless it's too fatty. Excess fat can cause weight gain, diarrhoea, and a disease called pancreatitis. Dogs shouldn't eat chocolate, grapes, or onions, either, for fear of damaging their heart, liver, kidneys, and blood. Many dogs also can't digest dairy, and scoffing down bones and corn-on-the-cob can harm their intestines.

the BEGGING STARE

"Poor baby. You want a piece of bacon?" Have you ever heard somebody coo to a dog like that? Maybe you've even done it yourself. But be strong. Don't cave! That sweet little beggar sitting by your chair and staring directly at you while you eat is not starving. What he is doing is controlling you.

A staring dog is communicating with you. He may be asking for the buttered roll on your plate, or maybe he's telling you he's the boss and you'd better not come closer. But if you sneak him a bite of bacon, he'll push his luck every time. He might even think you're well trained yourself and are letting him give all the orders! If you're a follower, he must be the leader. If he's the leader, then he doesn't have to listen to you. See where this is heading?

Here's how to handle a begging dog: ignore his staring. Don't give him any attention at all. Make sure that nobody else feeds him from the table, either. Eventually, the little scamp will realize you're in charge and that begging doesn't work. Then when you tell him to go lie down, he will probably do it!

Scientists say dogs are four times more likely to steal food when they think you're not looking!

JUST ONE PIECE. PRETTY PLEASE WITH GRAVY ON TOP?

Beagle

the CHALLENGE STARE

Nobody likes being stared at, and for good reason. Fierce hunters like wolves and tigers stare hard at their prey before they attack. So it's only natural that both humans and animals consider staring an unspoken threat.

In fact, staring makes humans so uncomfortable that we can sometimes sense it happening even when somebody is looking at us from behind. If we turn around and catch them in the act, we often respond by moving out of view. Or we get edgy and irritated. "Take a picture," we say. "It'll last longer."

Dogs react in equally unfriendly ways. Many can't handle being stared at by a human, even if the human's gaze is loving and admiring. The first thing the dog will do is look away. If the human still doesn't get it, the dog might actually turn away, presenting his backside to look at instead of his face.

Some dogs even engage in staring contests. Two dogs will look directly into each other's eyes and hold their gaze. Just like a human staring contest, the first dog to look away loses.

Dogs can see much better than we can. Although they see fewer colours in our spectrum, they visualize many more shades of grey.

Jack Russell terrier

Great Dane

EARS ERECT AND TEETH BARED

Scary, isn't it? It's supposed to be. A dog's only weapon is his teeth, and angry or threatened dogs curl their lips back to show them all. This makes the canines visible. These are the long fangs on each side of the upper and lower jaws that today's dogs have inherited from wolves. Wolves use them to grab and hold their prey when hunting.

A dog showing his teeth isn't always bad news, however. So look at the rest of his face and body. Whenever you see raised ears and a mouthful of teeth, watch out! That animal is giving a clear warning that he might attack. A dog most often shows this face to other dogs. He does it to prove he is strong and in charge, meaning he's the boss.

Trained guard dogs are the animals most likely to look this way around people. Some big and powerful breeds, such as Rottweilers, Dobermans, and pit bulls, have been bred to be strong and confident and to not show fear. It's their job to scare off intruders. So do as they say and leave. Back away—slowly and quietly.

A healthy adult dog has about 42 teeth, the same number as a wolf.

DR. GARY'S VET TIPS

VETS CAN tell a dog's age by looking in its mouth. We check for healthy gums and missing or discoloured teeth. Years of chewing wears down teeth, so we also look at how sharp they are.

Manchester terrier

PRICKED EARS

Pointy and floppy, short and long. Dogs' ears come in many different shapes and sizes. Pricked ears stand up straight and can be seen from a distance. They also rotate a little bit. Wild canines—wolves, foxes, and coyotes—all have pricked ears. Many pet dogs do, too. Just look at a Chihuahua or a Siberian husky. Ears like theirs are very expressive. It's almost as if a dog has a pair of miniature satellite dishes on top of his head. They go up and maybe a little bit forward when a dog is curious or interested in something. Why? Lifting his ear flaps is like opening the doors to his inner ear canals. That and tipping his head in the direction of the sound help a dog pick up even the faint scurrying of a mouse behind a wall.

Dogs don't hear everything better than humans, but they can detect a wider range of sounds. Sound is measured in vibrations per second (vps). The higher the number of vibrations, the more high-pitched the sound. Humans hear about 20,000 vps. Dogs can hear up to 100,000 vps. Some police dogs are trained to respond to a so-called silent whistle. It makes a very high-pitched sound that dogs can hear, but human criminals can't.

Dogs can hear noises that are up to **four times** farther away than those humans can hear.

Welsh corgi

Labrador mixed breed

the SUBMISSIVE GRIN

According to an old song, when humans smile, the whole world smiles with them. Unfortunately, that's not true for dogs. When Buddy pulls back his lips and shows his teeth, most people turn tail and run. They don't bother to check out his ears, which are down and pulled back. Nor do they consider whether he's meeting a stranger or defending a bone. And that makes all the difference. We must consider the situation when an animal "talks" to us, and we can never go by one sign alone.

An open mouth that turns down at the corners is called a "submissive grin". It's an instinctive behaviour that runs in families. Some dogs do it out of habit, others when they're feeling uneasy. For some reason, dogs rarely grin at other dogs. They only grin at people, and big dogs seem to do it more.

Of course, that only compounds the problem. A mean owner who misreads a dog's expressions might end up mistreating a sweet, gentle canine. And all because of a smile.

A dog can make about 100 different facial expressions.

Boston terrier

DR. GARY'S VET TIPS

ENGLISH SPRINGER SPANIELS, bloodhounds, Weimaraners, and golden retrievers don't hear as well as dogs with pricked ears. How can they? Their outer ears are so long and floppy, it's like they're wearing earmuffs—velvety soft earmuffs that feel delightful to touch!

I'LL BE NICE, IF YOU'LL BE NICE. DEAL?

American Eskimo–Pit bull mix

FRIENDLY PINNED-BACK EARS

A dog might pull her ears back so that they almost appear pinned to the side of her head. To be sure how she's feeling, you need to read the rest of her face, too. If she isn't showing any teeth and there are no wrinkles above her nose or between her eyes, this is a good sign. The dog is either acting submissive or friendly. Either way, she means you no harm.

Sometimes, trouble comes when a dog has long, heavy ears that hang below its chin. A cocker spaniel or basset hound simply can't pull its ears back. They won't go! These dogs can't "talk" as well as a pointy-eared German shepherd can. People like the puppyish look of soft, floppy ears, so they have deliberately bred dogs with ears of that shape. Floppy-eared dogs do still change the positions of their ears according to how they feel. But the differences are very subtle. We (and other dogs) have to look closely to see what they're saying.

Hearing loss can be inherited and is common in dogs with white coats. One in five Dalmatian puppies is born permanently deaf.

YAWNING

Yawning means your dog is tired, right? Not necessarily. The reasons dogs yawn are more tied to stress than lack of sleep. Sometimes, dog obedience teachers find their whole class yawning. That's because inexperienced dog owners can sound cross, and hounds get upset. Unsure about what they're supposed to do, the dogs yawn. It calms their nerves.

To see how it works, stretch and force yourself to yawn. Doesn't that feel relaxing? Besides trying to calm themselves, dogs yawn to reassure other dogs that they mean no harm. They might even yawn to prevent a fight.

Yawning is contagious. People "catch" yawns from each other. And dogs "catch" yawns from people. Really. A Portuguese scientist says half the dogs she studied yawned when they heard a human yawning. When the yawning voice belonged to their owner, that made the dogs five times more likely to yawn, too.

Now yawn again, this time with your pooch listening. Does Mr. Pickles join in? If so, that's great. He shares your feelings and is emotionally attached to you.

Shih tzus

The roof of the mouth of shar-peis and some Saint Bernards is black. Chow chows and shar-peis even have **black gums** and tongues.

Chow chow

AHH!
THAT WAS
AS RELAXING
AS A DAY
AT THE
DOGGIE
SPA!

LICKING YOUR FACE

When Rusty slurps you on the face, is he giving you a doggie kiss? Sure, he could be, especially if he knows doing this makes you happy. But, to dogs, this is also considered an "appeasement gesture". Dogs inherited this cute but sloppy behaviour from their wolf ancestors.

A wolf mum hunts for her supper and carries her kill home in her stomach. But the minute she gets there, her hungry pups lick her muzzle and lips until she throws the food all back up! Then the pups devour that icky mess of already-chewed meat. Yuck! Somebody else's partly digested food doesn't appeal to us. But young pups find it goes down much easier.

Domestic dogs usually outgrow this behaviour. But an adult dog will go back to it when he's licking, er, sucking up. This furry con artist thinks that by acting puppyish and "cute", he can sweet-talk you into giving him anything he wants. And he's probably right, unless you're wise to his game!

A dog licking his own nose and lips may also be nervous or anxious. Maybe you're scolding him, or an aggressive dog has entered his space. Lip licking is the nervous dog's way of calming himself. It's called a "displacement" behaviour. In this case, it's a "calming signal" and shows the world he doesn't want to fight.

A boxer named Brandy holds the record for the longest tongue on a dog— 17 inches (43 cm)!

Papillon

55

WHAT IS THIS DoG SAYING?

The Scenario

Judy is a superactive rescue dog. She heads outside to play and run, but she never takes her eyes off her owner. Judy's owner became concerned and wondered if her dog's staring was normal. Then there's Hershey, a beautiful chocolate Lab, who never stops looking up at his owner when he's seated at the dinner table. His owner wondered if there was any possible reprieve from that stare.

You Be the Expert

So what's going on inside Judy's and Hershey's heads? What do their stares mean?

Dr. Gary gets questions about dog stares all the time. For Judy, she wants her owner in her sights at all times. This is common with shelter dogs who have been lost or abandoned at some point in their lives. She feels insecure.

Though flattering, Judy's constant fixation on her owner is unhealthy. As a full-grown adult, Judy should be able to show some independence, especially when playing with other dogs. She should be able to relax and trust that her owner will still be there.

Now, if you've ever eaten with a dog sitting at your feet, you know what Hershey wants. Food! Hershey figures he just has to sit quietly and focus his big brown eyes on his loving people. Most of the time food will magically, if not so mysteriously, be handed to him. Works every time!

Talking to Your Dog With Your Eyes

Among friends, a stare is harmless. Your dog is telling you he wants something, and the fact that he feels free to ask means your relationship is working!

When you gaze at your dog, he can read your feelings by looking at your eyes. Such open communication between you and your canine is a great way to bond.

But when your dog becomes overly attached, serious anxiety can develop. Suppose Judy's owner wants to spend a weekend away. Judy might go berserk and bark non-stop or chew the woodwork.

You can keep your relationship healthy by helping your dog see the world as a welcoming place. Boost her confidence by introducing her to new dogs, activities, people, and places. Then try leaving her home alone. Give her toys and stay away only minutes at first. Gradually lengthen the time. Eventually, she'll trust that you will return.

But what about Hershey and his begging stare? Ignore it! Check out pages 40–41 for details, but never, never, never give in. If you do, you'll lose his respect.

So, go ahead and enjoy a silent talk with your furry friend. Just pay attention to what each of you is really saying.

TIME TO PUT THAT BOTTOM ON THE GROUND!

Teaching your dog "sit"

 1 Capture your dog's attention with a treat—food or her favourite toy. Hold the treat near her nose. Then move it over her head and back toward her tail.

 2 As she follows the treat with her eyes, she'll lower her bottom. The minute it hits the floor, say "sit". Use a firm tone of voice.

 3 Praise your dog! Stroke her back and give her the treat.

 4 Say "OK" or "all done" enthusiastically, and let her get up and move around.

 5 Practise this exercise several times daily, but if either of you gets frustrated or tired, make sure to stop and pick it up again later.

For a dog, learning to "sit" is a basic skill. But dog training takes patience. And you must be consistent. Always speak the same words in the same tone of voice.

colate Labrador
iever

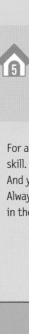

Shih tzu

Rhodesian ridgeback

THE NoSE KNOWS

SMELLED ANY GOOD STORIES LATELY? Your dog has. Dogs are fur-coated sniffing machines. We humans remember some smells, but people mostly rely on their eyes to interpret the world, and we store our memories in the form of words.

Dogs sniff. A dog has a special pouch in the roof of his mouth for storing smells. And his brain is like a giant database full of searchable odours. Dogs pick up thousands of smells, many of which we can't even detect.

You probably like the nose you have. But if you traded with your dog, here's what you'd get: a supersensitive schnozz with about 40 times more scent cells, a much larger brain area devoted to cataloguing smells, and the ability to wiggle your nose. Dogs can wiggle each nostril independently to figure out what direction a scent is coming from.

If you had all that, you could ride in a boat like Cloud the Labrador retriever and help find lost dolphins. Or you could prowl the forests of Cambodia sniffing for tiger poo. Not interested? Thank goodness we have dogs.

BOTTOM-SNIFFING

No doubt about it! Dogs sure have a weird way of saying "hello". Instead of shaking paws, they sniff each other's rear ends! One dog stands perfectly still and lets the other one sniff him. Then they switch positions so that both animals get a turn.

Actually, there is good reason for this. A dog's anal glands are located in its bottom, and those glands give each hound a signature scent. Dogs don't recognize each other by name, or even by looks. They identify friends by the way they smell.

To a dog, another canine's personal smell carries as much data as an ID card. These data tell if a dog is healthy or sick, young or old, and even what he ate for dinner.

Puppies that stay with their mothers for at least seven weeks usually know the ritual. Their mum has taught them. But puppies that are taken away too soon might take offense when some strange mutt starts sniffing around. Any dog that refuses to cooperate with the rear-end courtesy is considered "rude" and will find it hard to make doggie friends.

NICE TO MEET YOU! GO AHEAD AND TAKE A GOOD WHIFF.

Beagle

Puppies are born deaf and blind, but quickly learn to identify their mother solely by smell.

Dachshund

GOSSIP HOUNDS

Dogs can't text or use the Internet, but they still keep track of what's going on. How? By smell. When on a walk, dogs sniff all the spots where other dogs have peed or pooed. The information they get is like reading a Facebook newsfeed. Imagine a dachshund named Milo patrolling his neighbourhood:

Izzy came by this morning, Milo thinks, sniffing the grass. *She was feeling sad, so maybe her owner is away.* He sniffs a fire hydrant next. *That show-off Tramp acts like he owns the place.* Milo lifts his leg and sprays higher up on the hydrant than Tramp did. *Humpf,* he snorts. *That'll show him I'm the boss.* By the end of his route, Milo is up-to-date on the canine news.

Marc Bekoff, a University of Colorado scientist, wondered if dogs know their own smell. To find out, he spent five winters labelling and mixing up patches of yellow snow and studying his dog's reaction. Turned out that when Jethro sniffed his own urine, he walked on by. But when the urine belonged to another dog, Jethro peed over it.

Sometimes dogs scratch the ground with their hind feet after they go for a number two; they do it to stir up the scent and mark their territory.

HMM. LOOKS LIKE BO AND RITA ARE BACK TOGETHER.

Dachshund

SNIFFING BETWEEN YOUR LEGS

It is soooo embarrassing. You go to a friend's house and their dog comes up and sticks his nose between your legs. It's enough to make your face burn redder than a tomato. But before you totally lose it, try to remember that the annoying mutt doesn't mean to be rude. He's just being nosy. And his actions are considered perfectly polite in Dogville. Like it or not, dogs are terrific at identifying people—only they don't just do it by looks—they do it by smell.

And smelling between your legs makes good sense. We humans have lots of sweat glands down there. These glands produce chemicals that are packed with information. One good sniff tells a dog who you are, where you've been, and whether or not you live with any other animals. He can also determine if you're healthy or sick and even what you ate for supper. Of course, if it was chili or garlic bread, that's not a secret anyway. Anybody have a mint?

Some dogs use their sense of smell to help find people buried in avalanches.

DR. GARY'S VET TIPS

EVER TRY to hide your feelings from your dog? You can't do it. When we're afraid or excited, we give off chemicals in our sweat. It depends on the individual, but some dogs can smell these changes. Your hound really can smell fear!

ROLLING IN THE STINK

Eww. Poo stinks! Yet dogs love to roll in the icky stuff. Nobody really knows why, but scientists have a couple of theories.

Some think that dogs do this to bury the disgusting smell under their own odour. Another idea is that the dog is trying to disguise himself. Thousands of years ago, wild dogs had to hunt and scavenge for their supper. This would be easier to do if the deer or whatever prey they were hunting couldn't smell the dog pack coming. Rolling in deer dung or a rotting animal carcass might mask their doggie smell, making it difficult for prey to detect them. For dogs, who see with their noses, changing the way they smell might be the canine version of dressing in camouflage.

But what might be the best idea is much simpler. Humans enjoy splashing perfume and aftershave on themselves, and they like smelling it on others. Maybe dogs like to smell good, too. The only difference is they prefer the scent of "eau de cow dung" to "lily of the valley".

An outdoor lamppost in Cambridge, Massachusetts, U.S.A., is the first streetlight ever powered by dog poo.

DR. GARY'S VET TIPS

IF YOUR dog has a tendency to roll in fox poo, help is now on hand to get her smelling nice again. Fox poo shampoo is specially designed to remove the foul smell from your pooch's coat. Simply follow the instructions on the bottle and she'll be sweet-smelling again in no time.

AHH! I LOVE THE DELIGHTFUL SCENT OF "EAU DE COW DUNG".

Lab mix

German shepherd

THAT IS DEFINITELY NOT PYJAMAS IN THERE!

PROFESSIONAL SNIFFERS

Worried about bombs, drugs, or an escaped criminal? What about peanuts (if you are allergic) or bedbugs? Whatever it is, you can bet there's a dog for that! Trained detection dogs alert humans to many hazards. Now they're even being trained to sniff out deadly cancers.

To understand how they do it, think about walking into the kitchen and finding a tray of chocolate chip cookies still warm from the oven. Mmm, we think. Those cookies smell good.

But a dog wandering into the same kitchen will smell more than cookies. He'll smell sugar, flour, eggs, chocolate chunks, and vanilla—every ingredient used in making them.

Scientists discovered that many tumours produce telltale chemicals. Given samples of people's breath, skin, or urine, a trained dog can break down each of these odours into all of its parts. He'll sniff every sample and sit if he smells cancer in any of them. So far, hard-working pooches have found cancers of the skin, bladder, lung, and breast. And they've found them early, when the disease is easiest to treat and cure.

A dog can smell half a teaspoon of sugar dissolved in an Olympic-size swimming pool full of water.

PIDDLING ON YOUR FEET

Name, rank, and serial number. That's the information soldiers are trained to give if they're captured by the enemy. And that's what a pet dog is trying to tell you when she says "hello" by piddling on your feet. It's not that Angel is so excited she can't hold it in, like people often think. She's peeing on purpose, to let you know that she knows her place.

Dog packs are like an army. They're organized in pyramid style, with every member assigned a rank. In the army, most soldiers are privates. In a dog pack, most dogs are born followers. Privates and followers occupy the lowest rank and are on the bottom of the pyramid. Generals and pack leaders stand at the top. They make decisions and tell everyone else what to do.

Unlike competitive people, most dogs don't mind having a low rank, as long as they have a strong leader to follow. By peeing on your feet, Angel is saying you are her leader. She is leaving you a smelly puddle to sniff that tells her age and gender and says she's going to follow your lead. Too bad our loyal canine followers don't just salute instead.

DR. GARY'S VET TIPS

IF YOUR DOG pees in the house, people used to say to rub her nose in it. But that's a myth. It doesn't help and just makes the dog afraid. Next time she might sneak away and pee in your wardrobe instead.

Children with dogs miss fewer days of school and may develop stronger immune systems.

I HOPE YOU UNDERSTAND I MEAN THIS IN A GOOD WAY.

Beagle

WHAT IS THIS DoG SAYING?

The Scenario

Dusty, a five-year-old German shepherd, is a sniffer dog. Dusty is learning to sniff out three strong aromas—birch, anise, and spearmint—all hidden in 30 different boxes. The boxes are paired with Dusty's favourite treats. Every time Dusty "alerts" on the right box, he gets the treat inside. Eventually, he learns to recognize the scent because he associates it with yummy snacks!

You Be the Expert

What makes a dog like Dusty such a good sniffer? Why does law enforcement depend on these dogs so much?

Dogs can sniff out contraband, such as illegal drugs at airports, make trains safe for passengers, find people who have been injured in fires or other disasters, and smell out the cleverest thief or drug smuggler. And they can do it all before we humans can even get the search started.

Dog noses are 40 to 100 times more sensitive than our noses and have many fine hairs, or cilia, which help move scent molecules quickly through the nostrils. The molecules head down twisty nasal passages that extend down a long tunnel in the muzzle, until they hit the olfactory nerve, which runs straight to the dog's brain (ours does, too). Dogs have many more of these twisty nasal passages than humans, so they can sort and identify smells much better and faster than we can. All dogs excel at sniffing, but some are champions at it. This makes these dogs perfect for jobs in law enforcement, drug investigations, search-and-rescue, and security services.

German shepherd

Passing the Test

Personality is the key to finding the best sniffers for the job. Prerequisites include five things: a deep desire to bond with people, athletic ability, food motivation, intelligence, and an ability to focus. Sniffer dogs are some of the most focused canines you'll meet. For an important search, such dogs have to be trained consistently to smell an odour, such as torn, dirty clothing. Plus, they have to be unfailingly rewarded with their favourite treats whenever they find the hidden clue.

Smells are a huge part of every dog's life. When you're a dog, there is no judgment, just scents, packed full of data, usually with no negative associations. Of course, some smells are unpleasant or even painful to dogs because of their strength, such as citrus, ammonia, or bleach. But dogs don't turn up their noses, like humans, at the smell of rot or sweat. Dogs find all smells interesting!

Not all dogs make good detectives like Dusty. But lucky for us some of them do. It's hard to imagine our lives without them.

Dachshund

TeLLING TAiLS

NERVES AND BONES, tendons and muscles. That's what your puppy dog's tail is made of. It's actually part of his spine and is more important than it looks. That's because dogs' tails are made for "talking".

And that is what they do, except a few breeds that don't have tails. Their tails are docked, or shortened, soon after birth. Why? Docking prevents hunting dogs from injuring their tails, say some breeders. But the truth is that docking isn't necessary. It's just done for looks, and a dog can't use a short stump to communicate. A dog that can't communicate has a harder time making friends with other dogs. And we humans have to look harder to understand what a dog with no tail is trying to tell us.

Some try for a high-tech solution. Dr. Roger Mugford, a British dog expert, invented a small sensor that you can strap to a dog's tail. Called a wagometer, it measures the number of wags, how close together they are, and how big they are—three clues to how a dog is feeling.

Luckily, you don't need a wagometer. Keep reading to learn to recognize the different kinds of wags and what each one means. Believe me, it's quite a tail, er, tale.

Weimaraner

the SHOWY TAIL

Suppose you were a battlefield general and you wanted to rally the troops before the days of mobile phones or even walkie-talkies. Well, what many old-time generals did was to raise a flag. Troops seeing the flag would know exactly where the general was and that they should join him.

Wolf parents and lead dogs do the same thing. Only they don't raise flags. They raise their tails. A dog strutting around with his tail held high is showing the world he is in charge.

This works even better if the lead dog has a tail that is easy to see. Maybe that's why wolves have big bushy tails and many dogs have tails with lighter-coloured hair on the underside. The light colour shows when their tails go up. A perfect signal flag!

A dog's tail should never be pulled. Pulling it could dislocate the bones and cause nerve damage. Then it won't move anymore.

Golden retriever and chocolate Labrador retriever

Shepherd–pit bull mix

IF YOU have a Doberman pinscher, Rottweiler, or other large dog with a docked tail, you might want to stay away from the dog park. These dogs can't raise their tails to warn other dogs that they're feeling irritated. So they might get into fights.

I'M WARNING YOU. STAY OUT OF MY TERRITORY.

Yellow Labrador retriever

the STIFF, HIGH TAIL

Different kinds of dogs carry their tails differently, depending on their breed. A sled dog naturally holds his fluffy tail so high that it curves all the way over his back. So does an Alaskan malamute. But this is not true of collies, Labrador retrievers, or many other dogs. These dogs let their tails hang down like ponytails.

The thing to remember is this: The more afraid a dog is, the lower his tail goes. When he's feeling friendly and relaxed, he will carry his tail in the normal position. If he raises his tail any higher than that, he's feeling right sure of himself. And if his tail is held both high and stiff, watch out! That dog is on guard. He may even attack!

Human ancestors had tails. When we started walking upright, our tails shrank to just "tail bones".

Lab mix

the CROOKED TAIL

A crooked little dog had a crooked little tail, and they ended up together in a crooked doggie jail. That might be silly and fun in a children's nursery rhyme. But in real life, not so much. You know how some kids can hold their index finger out straight and just bend the tip? They're able to do that because they're double-jointed. But the reason they do it is to see you squirm.

Some dogs can do the same thing with their tails. Trouble is that when they do, uh-oh. Far from being a cute trick, it's a danger sign. This is another behaviour that seems to have been passed down from wolves, and any dog that does it has bad things on his mind. It could be he hears a strange noise or sees a person or dog he doesn't know coming toward him. Whatever it is, he thinks it's a threat, and he's preparing to defend himself. So don't get involved. You don't want him to mistake you for the enemy!

An animal rescue organization gave Scooter, a pit bull once used in muggings by criminals, a second chance. Today she's a licensed therapy dog.

Puppies don't begin wagging their tails until they're about seven weeks old. That's the age when they start "talking".

Shetland sheepdog (Sheltie) mix

the SCARED WAG

You might think a wagging tail is a sure sign that a dog is friendly. Not always! Dogs also wag their tails when they are scared, feeling uncertain, or even ready to bite. Look closely at a dog's wagging tail. Is it held high and stiff with just the end wagging? The wagging could be very slow, or the tip of the tail could be jerking back and forth so quickly that it almost looks like it's vibrating. Either way, that dog is neither happy nor friendly. He's nervous and upset. Maybe he's protecting his favourite chew toy or has his eye on a rabbit.

The best thing you can do is nothing. Don't try to stroke him. In fact, don't even approach him. That might scare the dog into attacking and biting you. Just back away and leave him alone. Later, when his tail is back in its normal position and wagging broadly, you can try to make friends.

BACK OFF!
I NEED
MY SPACE.

the TUCKED TAIL

A dog's tail is like a mood ring. It shows how he's feeling. Only a dog's tail doesn't change colour to do it. It changes position, or shape, or the way it moves.

Tails started out as a way to help a dog keep her balance when running superfast. Leaning into turns throws a dog's weight to one side. To keep from falling over, a dog evens the weight by throwing her tail to the opposite side. Retrievers also use their tails like rudders when swimming. It helps them turn. But suppose the dog is just out for a stroll. Is that heavy tail dragging behind and doing nothing? Nope. Over time, the tail has developed another use—as an emotional signal.

If a dog's tail is down and tucked between her hind legs, the message is clear. This canine is scared! Maybe she hears thunder booming or sees a bigger dog coming down the street. Or it might be you're angry, and she's afraid of you.

Mood rings are just for fun. But a dog's tail always tells the truth.

A Japanese company invented a furry, clip-on tail for people, controlled by brain waves. The tail **wags** when you're happy and **droops** when you're sad.

YIKES! THAT NOISE SCARES ME SILLY.

DR. GARY'S VET TIPS

DIFFERENT DOGS have different kinds of tails. A keeshond's tail curls over his back. A whippet carries his between his legs. So how do you know what your dog's relaxed tail position is? When people adopt from our shelter, we show them how their dog's relaxed tail looks. Then whether his tail is high or low can be based on that position.

Nova Scotia duck-tolling retriever

the STRAIGHT TAIL

Who? What? When? Where? Why? That's what everyone—both human and canine—wants to know. In fact, you might be surprised at all the sights, sounds, and smells that capture a dog's attention. Even a mutt that's snoring up a storm can spring to life at the sound of approaching footsteps or the smell of a roasting marshmallow. Dogs descended from wolves, after all, and wolves depend on their keen senses to survive.

One sign that a dog is interested in something is a straight tail raised level with her back and pointing away from her body. It's true she may hold her tail higher than normal. But that's okay, as long as her tail isn't stiff. And it's fun to watch what makes dogs take notice.

Would you believe some of them like TV? Yep. Most dogs used to ignore it. But that is changing with the new high-tech, flat-screen televisions, which have a much clearer picture. Now hounds are becoming fans. They especially like nature shows and shows starring . . . dogs!

Californians can subscribe to DogTV, the first cable television channel offering 24/7 programming designed especially for dogs. Canines living elsewhere can watch the channel online.

Shepherd-Lab mix

Chiweenie

the HAPPY WAG

Thump! Thump! Thump! Your dog is lying down and wagging his tail against the floor. Or maybe he's standing and whipping his tail wildly back and forth. He may even wag it in circles.

Dogs wag their tails because they're excited, and Rosie is excited, for sure. She's happy to see you. But not all wags are the same. Dogs also wag their tails when they're feeling aggressive or afraid. How can you tell which is which, especially when you're meeting a dog for the first time?

First, think about how you wave to a friend. If you really want her to notice you, you wave big. A dog wanting your attention does the same. Her tail moves in a wide arc, making the wag large and sweeping. Next, look at the speed. If it's fast, smile. That dog really loves you.

Scientists recently discovered something else. It's hard to see because dogs move around so much. But guess what? Happy dogs always wag to their right!

DR. GARY'S VET TIPS

A WAGGING tail is a truth-ometer. Dogs can't control when or how wagging happens. The tail is like an electric line connected directly to the brain that transmits how a dog is feeling.

Dogs only wag their tails to people and other animals. They don't wag at trees, cars, or anything that can't respond.

WHAT IS THIS DoG SAYING?

The Scenario

Brew, a Labrador retriever, is a 40-kilo tail-wagging machine. The big, yellow dog wags at well-meaning strangers he meets on the street. He wags if he thinks he's about to be fed. And his tail wags faster than windscreen wipers in a hurricane when his family comes home.

But Brew also wags when he's feeling uneasy. He even wags when he's picking a fight with other dogs. All this nonstop tail wagging confused Brew's owner, who finally called Dr. Gary and asked, "What's up with my dog's crazy tail?"

You Be the Expert

So what exactly is Brew trying to tell us with his tail? Does a wagging tail mean more than one thing?

You can't speak dog without speaking tail. That's just all there is to it. A wagging tail is a sign of excitement. But there are two kinds of excitement—happy excitement and nervous excitement. When Brew is greeting his family or expecting a bite of bacon, he's feeling happy excitement. At those times his tail wags wildly from side to side or even twirls in a circle.

Brew's feelings change when other dogs cross his path. He's excited, for sure, but in a nervous way. Is this strange dog going to act friendly and nice, or he is a bully? Unsure of the dog and unsure of himself, Brew's tail wag slows down. It's his way of saying, "I think I'm happy to see you, but let's take it slow." Or it may speed up! A stiff, high tail that wags or vibrates just at the tip means, "Watch it, buddy.

Jack Russell terrier

You're no friend of mine." A few dogs, including Jack Russells, Shiba Inus, basenjis, and American Eskimos, always hold their tails high. But with most dogs, the higher and stiffer they hold their tail, the more aggressive they are feeling. They lower it when they're feeling afraid.

Learning Dog Wags

Even if you cross paths with a sweet dog like Brew, you still have to ask the owner for permission to stroke the dog. This dog is probably wagging his tail energetically straight out and back and forth. You think he's happy and that he wants to see you, and you're usually right. But always ask before approaching any dog, because even a "happy" tail wag may not always mean that dog is happy about you.

There are lots of tail shapes and lots of tail positions and movements. It's important not to get caught up in exactly where the tail is and how fast or slow it's wagging. When you see a dog, stop and think about what your first feeling about that dog is. Are you comfortable or cautious? That's exactly how dogs think, too. Learning to speak dog is as much about feeling as it is about looking and listening.

When sizing up a dog, always listen to your gut. Brew does.

SIMON SAYS STAY RIGHT THERE!

Teaching your dog "stay"

 1 This command is much easier to teach after your dog learns "sit". See page 57.

 2 Stand in front of your dog and ask him to sit.

 3 When he sits, put your palm flat out in front of him like you're indicating him to stop, and say "stay".

 4 Take one step backward and say "Stay." If your dog is still in the same position for a minute or two, praise him and give him a treat.

 5 Make sure to praise your dog when he is in the "stay" position, not after he has moved. He may think he's being rewarded for moving.

 6 Enthusiastically clap and say "OK" to release him from the position.

Alaskan Klee Kai

Gradually increase your distance, and even turn your back to him and walk into the next room. Soon, your dog will be the perfect example of obedience!

HoUND SOUNDS

WISH THOSE BARKS were in human language? Several companies sell gadgets that claim to translate Buddy's barks, yips, and whimpers into people speak.

In Japan, dog experts recorded actual dog barks and grouped them according to six emotions. All the sounds are stored in a computer database. To translate, you attach a special radio microphone to your hound's collar and keep the receiver with you. When your dog barks, the device matches his sound to one in the database and sends you a text message. "I need a friend," it might read. Or, "I'm ready to play." The original Bowlingual was such a hit that now you can download it as an iPhone app.

Who needs a translator anyway? A Hungarian research study showed that kids are especially good at interpreting doggie sounds. Even babies can match happy and angry barks to pictures of happy and angry dogs.

So forget the gadgets. Your dog would probably prefer treats to texts anyhow.

Samoyed

Spaniel-shepherd mix

RAPID BARKING

Woof! Woof! Woof! A lot of rapid barking is an urgent call to gather the pack. If the barking continues but drops to a lower pitch, the dog is even more concerned. "Come quickly," he's saying. "There's something wrong." The problem could be a burglar, a house fire, or a child in distress. Or it could be nothing more than the postman coming up your garden path. But there is no way to know, unless you respond.

Just think of Mr. Darling, in the story of Peter Pan. Mr. Darling gets mad at Nana, the family's Newfoundland, and drags her out of his kids' bedroom. Then he ties her up in the garden. Poor Nana sees Peter arrive, and she barks and barks. But Mr. Darling ignores her. Later, he discovers his children are missing! Blaming himself for their disappearance, he brings Nana back inside and makes himself sleep in her kennel.

Silly? Yes. But it's always wise to answer a canine alarm call, because barking dogs have saved many lives.

Some dogs bark very fast.
One cocker spaniel was clocked barking more than 90 times per minute!

STUTTER BARK

Let's play ball! Or Frisbee! Tag or chase! It doesn't matter what the game is. The dogs could be collies, shih tzus, or who knows what. They might be boisterous puppies or full-grown adults. All the players could be dogs or maybe the line-up is canine against you. Whatever the ground rules, the invitation to play always sounds the same—it's a stutter bark.

A stutter bark has two parts. The end of the bark is louder than the beginning. It sounds like *arr-ruff*, and it sounds happy.

Playful dogs also make another joyful noise. They laugh! Canine chuckles are too high-pitched for humans to hear, and scientists used to dismiss the idea. But humans can hear the laughs on tapes made with special recording equipment. These laughs sound different from barks. They're more like breathy pants. They're also quite distinctive. Other dogs immediately recognize these doggie ha-has and can't wait to join in. An animal shelter in Washington State, U.S.A., sometimes plays a CD of the sound to help its caged dogs relax. All of us, including our pooches it seems, enjoy a good laugh!

The basenji, a dog from **Egypt**, doesn't **bark.** It **yodels** instead.

DR. GARY'S VET TIPS

MOST PEOPLE who give up their dogs to shelters say it's because they're moving away. But the real reason may be much different. Some dogs do take more work than others, which is why we have professional trainers. Good trainers are worth their weight in gold. For a fee, a trainer may even be able to take Misty away for a week or more to give her great focus time to work on commands. Then the trainer will return Misty, show you what she's learned, and explain the skills you need to make the relationship work.

COME ON. LET'S PLAY!

Greyhound mix

SLOW BARKING

We want dogs to bark. Their ability to warn us of danger is one of the things that brought humans and dogs together in the first place. But sometimes dogs drive us crazy with their noise. They bark and catch their breath, bark and catch their breath, for hours on end. And there's no reason for it—or so it seems.

But dogs are social animals. We bred them to hang out with us. Shutting up a dog alone in the house or tying him up alone outside is like a time-out to a kid. A dog with nothing to do and no one to do it with gets bored and lonesome. That annoying bark is its way of begging for attention.

One way to help with this problem might be to take your dog on a long, energized walk early in the day, before school or work. Then he might sleep while you're gone. If not, puzzle toys stuffed with food will help keep him busy. But the best way to deal with boredom is to have a dog walker come in to break up that long, lonely period during the day when you're not home. Doggie day care is another option. It can add up financially, but it's fun—like an all-day playtime for dogs.

Dogs are not the only animals that bark. Deer, California sea lions, and monkeys bark, too.

Maltese

Siberian huskies

HOWLING

Howling is a haunting, sorrowful sound. When wolves do it, in the woods after dark, some people quiver in fear. Others enjoy this call of the wild. But when domestic dogs sound off, there's no question about it. Everyone laughs or covers their ears!

Scientists think that wolves howl for several reasons. First, howling is like a wake-up call. Since wolves don't have bugles, they howl to wake up and gather their pack. Then there's the hunt. Hunting is dangerous; wolves can get hurt. So the pack howls before the hunt for the same reason football players chant or cheer before a game—to pump themselves up. They also howl to claim their territory and warn competitors to stay away.

When it comes to dogs, howling shelter hounds may be calling their owners. But many dogs seem to howl just for fun. One dog starts it off and others chime in. Pretty soon it's an all-dog jam fest, with every canine "singing" a different tune.

In 1980, a serious piece of music called "Howl" was performed in Carnegie Hall. It featured 20 human musicians and 3 howling dogs.

DR. GARY'S VET TIPS

HOWLING IS natural wolf behaviour that has carried over to dogs. The sound of violins, ambulance sirens, or harmonica music can stimulate some dogs to take part. Beagles are especially good at harmonizing!

BAYING

Baying sounds different from howling. A howling dog gets stuck on one note that he draws out forever. A baying dog changes notes. While howling dogs sound sad, baying dogs sound excited.

Hounds, like beagles and bassets, are great at baying. Hunters use them to track game. When the dogs pick up a scent, they go "on the chase". Trouble is, a dog's nose gets tired. After a few minutes, he'll "drop" the scent. It's like when you catch a whiff of perfume. The smell seems strong at first, but then it fades. That's why hunters run dogs in packs. When one dog drops the scent, another usually picks it up. Only animals still carrying the scent make any noise. Their baying tells the hunter where his dogs are and tells the dogs which hound to follow.

Humans breed hounds to have good voices. And some breeders claim they do better than that. They say their dogs actually sound different depending on whether they're after a rabbit or on to a deer.

It's likely that the beagle got its name from an old French word meaning "open throat", in honour of its loud baying.

Basset hound

GROWLING

Dogs bark much more than they growl. Thank goodness. Still, when a dog makes a deep, low sound from inside his chest, take him seriously. One of two things is happening. Either you and he are playing tug-of-war, and he's play-growling, or he's warning you to back off. Dogs are limited in the noises they can make, and growls all sound the same to us. Only the context, or circumstance, differs. That's why it's important to consider the context whenever a dog is "talking".

Generally speaking, the bigger the animal, the deeper its voice. Lions, tigers, and bears are huge, and they have ferocious, earthshaking growls to match. But that doesn't mean little animals can't growl. Harmless-looking rabbits and koalas do it. So do little dogs, like the Chihuahua, dachshund, and miniature poodle. They're trying to fool their enemies into thinking they are bigger than they are. And some lap dogs are quicker to bite than their hundred-pound (45-kg) cousins. So take any growl as a possible threat.

There is only one sound that dogs make that is even more dangerous than a growl. That is the sound of silence. If a dog has been growling at you and suddenly stops, don't think he is making friends. Once a dog decides to bite, he stops warning you and simply attacks.

Any noise dogs can make, wolves can make, too.

Rottweiler-shepherd mix

WHINING

Kids whine. Puppies whine. Lots of animal babies do. These high-pitched sounds are especially easy for animal mothers to hear. They're also extremely irritating, which makes them hard to ignore.

Puppies use whining the same way kids do—to get something they want. A whining puppy may want food to eat, someone to play with, or to come into the same room as you. She also could need to head outside for some bathroom business. There's even an off-chance she could be hurt or sick. Since there are so many things a puppy could be asking for, you can't just pretend not to hear her. Playing deaf won't work anyway. Puppies are persistent. They'll just whine louder and louder.

Adult dogs whine, too, and for all the same reasons. Any time an adult dog whines, she could be asking for something, she could be nervous and upset, or she could just be excited. So look around. See if you can spot what's exciting or upsetting her. It may be a person she doesn't know or a dog she wants to play with. Remove the threat, and your dog will thank you. Or toss the Frisbee in the other direction, and she'll probably forget all about it. She'll even stop making that persistent noise.

Puppies want **SO badly** to be with humans that when given a **choice** between going to a person and going to another dog, they **pick the human.**

MUM! I TOLD YOU, I WANT A SNACK.

Australian shepherd puppies

Shepherd mix puppy

WHIMPERING

A whimpering dog is like a crying child. It makes one of the saddest sounds you will ever hear. You can tell right away that the dog is hurt, sick, frightened, or in pain.

So it's no surprise that dogs can tell the same thing about us. Two scientists in London, England, had heard many stories about devoted dogs reaching out to comfort unhappy humans. But were the stories true?

To find out, they set up an experiment involving 18 dogs and their owners. One of the scientists would visit an owner at home. During the visit, the scientist and the owner did three things. They hummed. They talked. And they pretended to cry. Six of the dogs approached when they were humming, probably out of curiosity. But 15 came over when they thought the women were crying. Not only that, the dogs acted gentle and concerned. They tucked in their tails and bowed their heads. If dogs respond so quickly when we're suffering, shouldn't we do the same for them?

Lucky, a lost dog, survived ten days of below zero temperatures in the Italian Alps. A rescue worker heard whimpering and found him half-buried in snow.

Spaniel

UH-OH.
I'M REALLY
WORRIED
NOW.

PANTING

"Don't sweat it." We often say that to people who are stressing out over something. It comes from that wet-armpit feeling we get when we're nervous or scared. We sweat because feeling nervous makes our body temperature rise.

Dogs don't sweat. They can't. They don't have sweat glands all over their bodies like we do. Dogs have sweat glands only in the pads of their feet, which is why an overheated dog might leave a trail of wet pawprints behind.

Dogs do feel anxious, though. Just like us, anxiety makes their body temperature rise. So a very nervous dog sometimes does the same thing he does when it's a sweltering hot day or he's been running hard. He pants! He'll open his mouth and stick out his tongue to let water evaporate off the surface. As he does that, he'll make that familiar *hah, hah, hah* sound. It's called stress panting.

So if your dog does it, take him someplace where he'll feel safe. If you can't do that, then calm yourself and hope your energy rubs off on him.

DR. GARY'S VET TIPS

A DOG left locked in a car on a hot day can die from heatstroke in less than 20 minutes. The best idea is to not bring your hound to the shop at all.

Some dog breeds can run all day. Sled dogs in the famous Iditarod race run 1,110 miles (1,786 km) through the Alaskan wilderness.

WHAT IS THIS DoG SAYING?

The Scenario

There are some strange noises that come from our dogs, and not all can be easily interpreted. Dr. Gary got a call about Sparky, a dog that starts to loudly whine and squeak as soon as he hops into the car. Sparky is unstoppable. The car is a small, confined space, and no one can stand it! To his owners, Sparky sounds like he's in distress, even though he's headed for his favourite activity—a fun hike in the woods. There's nothing his people can do to make him stop making those loud and embarrassingly noticeable cries.

You Be the Expert

So what's going on with Sparky? Is he happy and excited, or is he stressed out and miserable about being in the car?

Dogs always tell us what they want and how they feel. They just use their own version of words. We have to take all of their body language and

Basset hound

the situation into account—the sounds are really just the accompaniment.

First, how does Sparky behave when his owner opens the car door? Does he stiffen up and try to run away, or does he hop right in? Next, consider how Sparky acts inside the car. We know he whines and squeaks, but what else does he do? It turns out that Sparky willingly jumps into the car. And once inside, he never sleeps. Instead, Sparky sits up straight, with ears perked, and stares out the front window. All his attention is focused on the road ahead.

This makes the diagnosis easy. Sparky is not distressed. All that noise he makes comes from happy anticipation. He is so excited that he can't hold it in. Lots of fun for Sparky, but a big headache for his people. And it's almost impossible to stop. But there are some great ways to help.

Barking Back
(or the closest we can get)

Tiring your dog with a walk or game of fetch before a car journey can help curb this kind of excited behaviour. Also, using something called a "calming cap" to cover your dog's eyes can keep him from overreacting. But, the truth is, dogs do want to speak!

There are many owners who feel as though their dog barks too much. Many dogs believe their job is to watch out for their owners. So, just remember that barking is done with the best intentions. These canines are letting us know that someone who might not belong is out there getting too close to the family. Yelling at your dog is not the answer. It takes a long time and a lot of work to decrease this "early-warning system," but try starting with something called "redirection"— using treats to reward him every time he's quiet in the car, when a dog walks by, or he doesn't run to the door. This isn't easy stuff, it takes work.

Dogs make lots of sounds: whining, crying, squeaking, barking, growling, chirping, trilling, and grunting. But just pay close attention, and you'll be able to translate in no time.

SOUNDING OFF

Tips to control excessive barking

 Dogs bark for many reasons. They might be bored, lonely, afraid, or trying to protect you and their territory.

 Give your dog plenty of exercise. A potty walk twice a day isn't enough exercise for most dogs. Take her out for a run. Fluffy also needs to exercise her brain to maintain a healthy lifestyle. Try playing games like Frisbee, tug-of-war, or fetch every day to stimulate her senses.

 Does Chance bark at everyone who walks by? Or big trees? He may just be trying to protect his space. Let him check out the object and reward him with words when he is quiet.

 Being home alone makes some pets anxious. Try leaving the TV or radio playing quietly to drown out some of that scary silence. Leave toys for your dog. Try sleeping with the toy for a night so it smells like you.

Canaan dog

TROUBLE TaLK

DOGS FOLLOW US AROUND and seem to feel what we feel. They get so close to us that it's hard sometimes not to think of our dogs as four-legged children. But dogs aren't humans. They're animals, with strong inherited needs and instincts that reach all the way back to their wolf ancestors.

Sometimes these instincts kick in, and our beloved pals do something weird. Whatever they do, it's usually something we consider dirty, annoying, or destructive. And then we get upset. "I can't stand it," you might say, when your dog keeps spinning after her tail. "Why won't she quit?"

If we can control our tempers long enough to stop and think, we'll realize that no creature on Earth tries harder to please than a dog. Whatever she is doing, she doesn't mean to be bad. There is a reason behind her strange behaviour. And you can bet she hopes that you'll figure it out.

Welsh corgi

EAR SCRATCHING

Itchy ears are not normal. All dogs scratch occasionally or shake their heads, but constant scratching means something is wrong.

Smell your dog's ears. Unless she has recently rolled in something disgusting, they should have a normal doggie smell. Now look inside. Is the skin scaly or thickened? What colour is it—a healthy pink, or red and angry-looking? You can also swab inside your pet's ears with a cotton ball. If the cotton comes out clean, that's good. But brown gunk on the cotton, a bad smell, and red skin all point to an ear infection.

However, just because everything looks and smells normal doesn't mean your dog is okay. She might have a compulsion, like some people who chew their fingernails. She could suffer from allergies (which are very common) or have something stuck in her ear. The only way to know is to take her to the vet. And don't delay, because scratching could mean more than an itch. Your dog might be in pain.

Timmy, a certified therapy dog who worked at ground zero, became hard of hearing. He was one of the first dogs ever to wear a canine hearing aid.

DR. GARY'S VET TIPS

WE SEE tail injuries all the time, especially in strong dogs with long tails that aren't well padded. Their tails get pulled, bitten, caught in doors, stepped on, and even smacked into walls and broken. We're constantly cleaning their wounds and wrapping them up so they can heal. A few inches of tubular foam-pipe insulation, bought at a DIY shop, makes a great tail bandage. Pull it open and fit it around the wound. Use medical tape to hold it on. But only leave it on for a day or so, or the wound will get infected and could cause even worse problems.

The world record for the longest dog tail goes to Bentley the Great Dane. His tail is more than two feet (0.6 m) long!

TAIL CHASING

Round and round the puppy dog goes. When she'll stop, nobody knows. The sad truth is probably never. Dogs that constantly chase their tails aren't playing a game, and they aren't having fun. Border collies, Shetland sheepdogs, and other dogs bred to chase and herd livestock have tremendous amounts of energy. If they don't have any real work to do, they may start chasing anything that moves. That includes bicycles, cars, and their own tails.

Tail chasing can quickly become an obsession. The dog doesn't want to do it, but she has to. She's driven to chase. She might even catch her tail and make it bleed. But she still can't stop. Even if a vet amputates her tail, she'll continue to chase the stump.

So what's the solution? Give her lots of regular exercise and some doggie toys. You could try swinging a ball on a rope and letting it fly. Running after that may help her to forget about her tail.

I'LL GETCHA!
I'LL GETCHA!

Akita mix

Greyhound-rottweiler mix

JUMPING UP ON PEOPLE

Humans often greet each other by hugging. Dogs usually sniff. But some submissive dogs say "hello" by jumping up and trying to lick your face.

This is babyish behaviour. It stems from puppyhood, when puppies smother their mums with licks. It's also a holdover from wolves, whose hungry babies lick their parents' mouths to make them throw up food for the pups to eat.

If dog owners equate these licks with kisses and act lovey-dovey when it happens, the behaviour will become a habit. Then the dog might jump all over unsuspecting guests who come to the door—and knock them flat on their behind.

Dog trainers suggest several ways of breaking the habit. You can block the jump by putting your hand in front of the dog's face. But the best way is to turn away and completely ignore him until he gets down. Whichever method you choose, start early, before Marley can reach your shoulders.

According to one survey, "jumping up on people" was the number one complaint cited by dog owners.

Scottish terrier

CHEWING the WOODWORK

Wooden windowsills, chair rungs, paper, and shoes don't look tasty to us. But dogs have teeth like wolves. They're designed to bring down prey, tear it apart, and crunch up the bones. Because of this, dogs feel an urge to chew.

Our lovable furballs have also been bred to be "man's (and woman's) best friend". So what is our good buddy to do if the whole family goes to work or school and leaves him home alone all day?

Combine killer teeth with boredom and loneliness, and you can get disaster. Dogs desperate for company may chew whatever they can reach. They also might bark non-stop or even go to the bathroom in the house. Luckily, there are fixes available. Give your dog plenty of durable chew toys. Some people give their pooches real bones, which many dogs love. But bones can splinter and poke holes in their gut. Even popular rawhide chews may pose a risk if given when the dog is unattended. The best answer is to avoid all real bones and not leave Dixie alone so much. There are plenty of other options: day care, hiring a professional dog walker, or even adding a companion kitty or another dog to the family.

"My dog ate my homework" is a favourite excuse given by school kids.

DR. GARY'S VET TIPS

THE STRANGEST thing I've ever removed from a dog's gut is a group of toy soldiers. But socks and underwear are the nonfood items most commonly eaten. That's a good reason to pick up after yourself, especially if you have a dog.

Basset-beagle mix

Pit-Lab mix

PEEING IN the HOUSE

Talk about exasperating. You leave your dog alone for an hour and come home to find a wet spot on the carpet. To begin with, take a deep breath. Control your temper and don't scold or punish your dog. It's too late anyway. He won't associate your scolding with peeing in the house. Then, clean up the mess. Use a chemical-based pet deodorizer or cleaner mixed with a little water to do it. Dogs tend to return to the scene of the crime. If you don't completely get rid of the smell, he's likely to go again in the same spot.

Understand that house-training a puppy takes time and patience. Most experts advise keeping a pup on a schedule, using a cage, and supervising him carefully whenever he's free. But suppose your pet is an older dog that suddenly starts having accidents. This could be a sign of illness. A urinary tract infection is one possibility, especially in female dogs. Diabetes is a second. So don't get mad at your dog. Take him to the vet instead.

DR. GARY'S VET TIPS

WE INTRODUCE cages to dogs (not just puppies) while they're still in the shelter. It helps traumatized and abused dogs gain confidence by giving them a safe haven or den. You can use a cage to train and calm your dog, too. Just be sure to let him out at least every four hours.

President Eisenhower's lively **Weimaraner** once **ruined** a White House rug worth **£16,000** by going to the bathroom on it.

I JUST CAN'T HOLD IT ANOTHER MINUTE.

Continental bulldog

Staffordshire terrier (pit bull)

EATING GRASS

Your dog isn't a cow, so why does she eat grass? Nobody really knows. Scientists think it may be an inherited instinct. Wild dogs sometimes get infected with worms that live inside their bodies. Eating plants or grass may help them get rid of these parasites by making them throw up.

But dogs don't always throw up after chomping on grass. In 2008, veterinarians at the University of California–Davis asked 1,600 dog owners about their pets' garden grazing habits. They found that fewer than one in four dogs throw up after nibbling grass. Most of the time, dogs eat grass like we eat salad. When they do spit up, it may be because they eat too fast and don't bother to chew the grass enough.

So the answer is that grass eating is normal for dogs. It won't hurt them, unless—and this is a big "unless"—the lawn has been treated with fertilizers, weed killers, or other chemicals, which could sicken your pet or worse. Keep him in gardens you know are safe. That probably means your own garden. You'll be a better neighbour, too!

Some of our prettiest flowers—azaleas, tulips, hyacinths, poinsettias, and lilies—are poisonous to dogs.

BUM-DRAGGING

Imagine you and a friend are watching TV, when . . . *eww!* Your dog sits and drags her bum right across the living room rug. Talk about gross! You'd probably burst out laughing or bury your face in the nearest sofa cushion.

Your poor dog doesn't mean to embarrass you. She might have an itchy bottom or even swollen anal glands. Anal glands give off a unique "perfume" that tells all the other dogs that Queenie is back in town or that Sir Richard was naughty today. When dogs ran wild, scent messages from these glands helped the dogs keep in touch.

Today's dogs are domesticated. They no longer roam freely over the countryside, so they don't really need these glands. But they still have them. And sometimes the glands fill up with fluid that makes them itch. So if Queenie scratches her bum in public, don't hide your head in shame. Just take her to the vet.

There are more pet dogs in the world—about half a billion—than human babies.

Pug

SORRY. BUT A DOG'S GOTTA DO WHAT A DOG'S GOTTA DO.

DR. GARY'S VET TIPS

PACKED ANAL glands aren't the only problem that causes a dog to drag its bum. Allergies or fleas also can be at fault. The important thing to know is that bum-dragging is a symptom of a medical condition; it will go away when properly treated. And a good, oatmeal-based shampoo can help a lot with itching!

French mastiff

WHAT IS THIS DoG SAYING?

The Scenario

Jane, a ten-year-old miniature schnauzer, is wonderful, fun, and loves people. But there's one problem—she loves people a little too much. Jane can't be left alone even at the San Diego Humane Society adoption centre, where Dr. Gary works. When she's alone she cries, jumps at the door, paces around her enclosure, and barks while waiting for someone to come and play with her. And if you know schnauzers, boy, can they bark!

You Be the Expert

So why does Jane go crazy when she's left alone? How can a dog like Jane learn to be on her own?

Just like you might miss a friend when you're away, your dog misses you, too. Your furry friend might cry or bark constantly when you leave, cause damage to the house or his cage, and may even hurt himself. Vets call these destructive actions "separation-related behaviours". Jane wants the

Miniature schnauzer

company of humans. She continues these upsetting behaviours until someone—anyone—comes and plays with her.

Supporting Your Dog

Sometimes these types of behaviours are diagnosed as "separation anxiety", but that's a term for a real behavioural illness that ultimately causes worry, anxiety, and some very specific ways of acting in a dog.

A dog may prefer to be with his people during the day. Like Jane, such dogs need a good workout routine, plus lots of stimulation and attention from their people. But separation anxiety is a serious problem. A dog with this illness has to be with people, and it doesn't matter whether he just went on a five-mile hike or played at the dog park, this dog cannot be left alone—ever.

Separation-related behaviours are difficult no matter if a preference issue or illness. All owners want their dogs to be happy and have full lives. The best way to ensure this is to make sure our dogs have jobs to do, with challenging playtime activities, and, if appropriate, other dogs to play and socialize with. Sometimes dogs need help from a vet for possible medications to decrease their stress. But most important, our canines need us to care for them to be sure they have the best lives possible.

YIKES! THAT'S ONE LOUD BARK!

Desensitizing your dog to thunder and fireworks

 Loud noises scare many dogs. Sometimes, a past bad experience makes them afraid, but many times the fear develops on its own.

 Create a safe zone for your dog. Pad and cover a box with soft blankets. Turn on a fan or radio near it when it's thundering to drown out some of the noise. Give her food and toys so she'll have a positive association with her "den".

 Distraction can also help some dogs feel better. When Princess gets anxious, whip out her favourite toy and coax her to play. Reward her for bringing back the toy or following your commands.

 Try enrolling in obedience class. Training might help boost your dog's confidence.

DoGGiE DEMEANORS

FOR A LONG TIME, scientists believed that humans were the only thinking, feeling beings on the planet. They thought dogs acted only on instinct.

But that view is changing. A researcher intrigued by his own dog's behaviour founded the Family Dog Lab, in Budapest, Hungary, and there have been many studies in recent years about the canine mind. People and dogs don't share much DNA, the tiny bits of hereditary material found in body cells. But it turns out that we do share something else equally important—similar brain chemistry. This makes dogs so tuned-in to humans that they're more than mind readers. They're mood readers.

Some experts still believe that when dogs reach out to comfort us, they're really trying to keep us alive so we'll take care of them. Yet there are so many emotional, gripping, and powerful stories from around the world of dog devotion. Could it be love?

Check out the next few pages to see how our devoted companions express other emotions.

CHECK OUT THE CANINES!

WANT TO SEE dogs in action? Check out these blue boxes on each page for web addresses for some of the best videos of dog emotion.

Springer spaniel

In Devon, England, a springer spaniel named Jess **bottle-feeds** orphaned lambs. The grateful lambs rub his **belly** in return!

I'M HAPPY AND RELAXED. ALL IS RIGHT WITH MY WORLD.

Basset hound

CALM AND RELAXED

Live dog or stuffed animal? When a real hound is completely relaxed, he almost looks stuffed. His whole body goes soft and still. When standing, he keeps all four feet flat on the ground. His tail is held like he normally holds it and may hang down in a gentle curve. It's neither stiff nor tucked between his legs. His ears stand up, but they don't tip forward. He's not showing teeth, and his tongue hangs loosely from his mouth, or his mouth is closed. This dog isn't a bit afraid. He feels as comfortable in his environment as you do in your bedroom at home.

But imagine you're a student facing a big test. Or maybe you're in the hospital facing major surgery. Or you're in a nursing home. You might also be the victim of a violent crime appearing in court to testify against your attacker. These are scary situations. They would make anybody nervous. But guess what helps to calm people down? A therapy dog.

Certified therapy dogs are the calmest of the calm. They snuggle up to troubled people. They lick their face and let them stroke their soft fur. People can endure a lot with an understanding dog by their side.

CHECK OUT THE CANINES!

CALM AND RELAXED therapy dogs help kids from Washington State, U.S.A., with the healing process at Seattle Children's Hospital.

FROM KING 5 NEWS:
http://tinyurl.com/
howtospeakdogrelaxed

CONFIDENT

Some dogs are shy. Others will go up to anyone. Some chase balls. Others lie at your feet. All dogs are individuals. Just like people, they have different personalities. It all depends on which traits a dog has inherited from his parents, his upbringing and training, and what his life has been like.

Rottweilers, German shepherds, and Doberman pinschers look big and strong. Bred as guard dogs, they were designed to be dominant—but not mean. "Dominant" is just another word for "confident". Everything about a confident dog projects that image— from him standing tall on stiff legs to his tail held high. His chest is forward and so are his ears. Dominant dogs strut. They are natural-born leaders. But size alone doesn't make a canine "top dog".

Consider Scooter, a miniature schnauzer. Scooter lives with Tina on a country road in Marcellus, New York, U.S.A. There are six big dogs, Newfoundlands and golden retrievers, in their neighbourhood. Whenever Tina takes Scooter for a walk, the neighbourhood dogs run out of their gardens to join them. One of these hounds weighs 186 pounds (84 kg). Scooter weighs 20 pounds (9 kg). But who goes first? You guessed it. Self-assured Scooter is the leader of that doggie play group!

There are three types of schnauzer. All three are identical, except for size—there's the miniature, the standard, and the giant.

DR. GARY'S VET TIPS

WE IN the animal welfare world are concerned about how people define the term "dominant". It's a characteristic, not a behaviour. People should not think it means bullying behaviour. Dogs instinctively follow the leader, the most confident dog in the pack. Just reward your dog for good behaviour, so he knows you're in charge, but then work together as a team.

Shepherd mix

JUST ME AND MY POSSE CHECKING OUT THE AREA.

CHECK OUT THE
CANINES!

WATCH AS Beagle Uno is crowned best in show at the Westminster Dog Show and becomes dominant Numero Uno!

FROM NBC SPORTS:
http://tinyurl.com/howtospeakdogdominant

Bernese mountain dog

FRIENDLY

Dogs may be the friendliest species on Earth. Given a chance, they will cozy up to elephants, cheetahs, even tigers. But no single sign can be trusted to tell you whether or not any one individual dog is friendly. A wagging tail isn't enough. Neither are perked ears or a calm mouth. You must look at the whole animal.

A friendly dog's whole body should be relaxed and loose. Downright wiggly, in fact. And her mouth? That should be soft-looking and open enough that you can see her tongue. Her tail should be wagging, but only fast, rarely slow. It might even turn in circles, like a windmill. Many friendly dogs are quiet. But if a dog is making noise, listen to her voice. Friendly dogs don't snarl or growl. They make short, high-pitched barks, whimpers, or yaps.

Scientists in Budapest, Hungary, say that we humans have custom-made dogs to love and depend on us. Because of this, humans and dogs are bonded like parents and children. They found that when dogs were anxious, nothing worked to calm them down—until a human sat beside them.

Every day for years, Ben the yellow Labrador retriever went swimming in the ocean with his best friend—a wild bottlenose dolphin.

DR. GARY'S VET TIPS

CUDDLING YOUR pooch may seem friendly to you, but that's not how it might feel to your dog. In fact, to a dog, this can be very forward and rude. Most dogs don't really feel comfortable with humans looming over them or holding them down. Besides, letting a dog lick your mouth could expose you to all the "wonderful" things that dogs lick. We'll leave it at that!

I LIKE YOU. DO YOU WANT TO BE FRIENDS?

CHECK OUT THE CANINES!

READ ABOUT and watch friendly canine Ben and Duggie the dolphin swimming like best buds on Tory Island off the coast of Northern Ireland.

DONEGAL COTTAGES BLOG, VIDEO FROM BBC:
http://tinyurl.com/howtospeakdogfriendly

German shepherd

ANXIOUS

Strange sounds, places, and people. Another animal. A trip to the vet. These things can stress out a dog. You can spot the signs. A suffering dog pulls her ears back and crouches lower to the ground. Her tail dips. Like an emotional thermometer, the lower it goes, the more anxious she feels. She might keep her mouth closed and whine. Or she could open it and rapidly pant. Sweat from her paws might leave splotches on the floor.

Your poor dog feels miserable, that's for sure. But you can help! First, remove whatever it is she's so concerned about. If you can't do that, move her instead. Take her for a good, fast walk to get her mind off things.

But the best thing you can do for an anxious dog is to take him for a good run, not just a leisurely walk. A recent scientific study showed that vigorous exercise causes a dog's body to produce endorphins. Endorphins are feel-good chemicals that can help a dog calm down and feel less stressed. If you can't run fast enough to keep up, play a 30-minute game of fetch or Frisbee with him instead. If you live near water, throw toys off the bank for him to retrieve. The point is to make the activity intense enough to cause an endorphin rush. And guess what? It's contagious: all that exercise will give your mood a happy boost, too!

Dogs that are being stroked produce fewer stress hormones than dogs that aren't being stroked.

DR. GARY'S VET TIPS

WHEN DOGS are really suffering, or the anxiety never goes away, we prescribe the same medicines taken by people. They often work very well, especially when combined with more exercise and play.

I DON'T UNDERSTAND WHAT'S GOING ON.

CHECK OUT THE CANINES!

A CONFIDENT (and fake) singing dog in an automobile accompanies a real tail-tucked anxious canine in this car commercial.

FROM YOUTUBE:
http://tinyurl.com/howtospeakdoganxious

Dachshund puppy

ALERT

Sleep well tonight. Your dog is "awake". Even when snoozing, a dog's senses remain on high alert. That's a good thing. In case of emergency, he'll bark an alarm. But anything from a footstep to the rumble of a car engine can catch a dog's interest.

She won't always bark. But she will sit or stand at attention, with her head held high. Her ears will be up and might be twitching. You can see her muscles tighten. Her mouth will be closed, and her eyes open wide. She might wiggle her nose as she sniffs the air. If her tail wags, it won't be stiff or bristling. She'll hold it straight out behind her or softly curled over her back.

Many dogs go on alert when they hear their owners come up or down the steps. But some hounds actually seem to have a "sixth sense". They can tell ahead of time when their owners are coming home. A British scientist conducted more than 120 videotaped experiments with a dog named Jaytee. Jaytee's owner could be a full five miles away, but the minute she headed home, he'd go to the window and wait—happy and alert.

In Italy, "lifedogs" leap from boats and helicopters and doggy paddle to swimmers in trouble. Swimmers grab a dog's harness and get towed to shore.

CHECK OUT THE CANINES!

SEE HOW this alert dog looks out for his military owner and the excitement at a reunion.

FROM YOUTUBE:
http://tinyurl.com/howtospeakdogalert

Pharaoh hounds

CHECK OUT THE CANINES!

THIS CUTE French bulldog gets a surprise cat attack and makes a very frightened noise!

FROM YOUTUBE:
http://tinyurl.com/howtospeakdogscared

WON'T SOMEBODY HELP? I'M REALLY SCARED.

Chocolate Labrador retriever

SCARED

We don't always know why dogs are afraid. It could be something as obvious as a more dominant dog entering their territory. Or it could be a hidden reason. This is especially true of shelter dogs. Someone may have mistreated them in the past.

Dogs learn by association. If you eat spaghetti and then become ill, you might come to associate the sight or smell of spaghetti with being sick. For a long while after that, you might refuse to eat it. The same thing happens with dogs. If a dog's former owner used to yank him and kick him whenever he walked on a lead, the dog might associate the lead with pain. Then when he sees you pick one up, he cowers or hides.

Fear is easy to spot if you know the signs. A scared dog pins back his ears so they won't be harmed during a fight. He lowers his tail and shows the whites of his eyes. His mouth will open, and he may pant or whine. Domestic dogs rarely get cold inside today's heated houses, so be alert for shivering or shaking. If it's a strange dog and he's afraid of you, move away. Never push an encounter, or the dog might bite. If the dog is yours, lead him through the scary thing. If he's afraid of the stairs, sit and bump down the stairs beside him. If he's afraid of the broom, squat and let him sniff it. Moral support from his favourite person may be all he needs.

DR. GARY'S VET TIPS

DOGS ARE often intimidated by tall people with deep voices. When I have a terrified dog on the examining table, I stroke him and speak softly to him. I also try to crouch down a little or sit on the floor with him.

Psychologist and dog expert Stanley Coren says dogs' greatest fear is "that you will not come back when you go out the door without them".

Golden retriever

PLAYFUL AND HAPPY

Like girls and boys, dogs just want to have fun. Only, with dogs, playing looks a lot like fighting. It can even sound that way, if one of the dogs play-growls. So how can you or the dogs tell the difference? Watch for an open mouth, waggling tongue, broadly wagging tail, and a play-bow.

Suppose Lulu wants to play. She'll ask Thor first with a quick bow and a bark. Then she'll dash away. Thor can chase her or not. It's up to him. But if he does run after, he's agreeing to follow the rules. The biggest rule is that nobody gets hurt.

If Thor accidentally bumps Lulu too hard, he'll do a quick bow. That tells her he's sorry and he wants to keep playing. Now Lulu can decide.

Want to try this yourself? Grab a tennis ball and call your dog. Get down on your hands and knees. Put your elbows and forearms flat on the floor, stick your bottom in the air, and smile. After all, you do look funny. Chances are your dog will bow back. Now play "keep-away". Part of the game is trying to trick each other, but don't forget: both you and your hound have agreed to play fair!

Owners who regularly play with their dogs develop a closer relationship with them.

CHECK OUT THE CANINES!

HOW CAN a deer resist a playful dog with a football?

FROM YOUTUBE:
http://tinyurl.com/howtospeakdogdeerplay

SEE THE play-bow in action as these two small dogs head out to play.

FROM YOUTUBE:
http://tinyurl.com/howtospeakdogplaybow

THREATENED

What makes a dog show his teeth? Often it's another dog or a stranger at the door. Dogs protect their territory, and dogs that spend little time around people as puppies are especially suspicious. There's a period between 3 and 12 weeks of age when puppies need to be handled a lot. And not just by one person. Puppies need a wide variety of "world experiences" to make them good canine citizens. New noises, sights, smells, and sounds all contribute to a well–rounded canine's education. Everyone in the family should pick up the pup. That gets him used to being touched by different people.

Puppies that don't get this handling grow up to be less friendly and more fearful. A threatened dog is afraid of you. But he is not so afraid that he won't defend himself. So he sends mixed signals. He lowers his body, tucks his tail between his legs, and folds his ears back. These are all signs of fear.

At the same time, he shows signs of aggression. As he tucks his tail, he raises his hackles. If the dog is short-haired, you can see a ridge of hair standing up along his spine. He wrinkles his nose and pulls back the corners of his mouth. To show he means business, he'll look you straight in the eye and bark loud and fast.

Take him at his word. More people are bitten by frightened dogs than by macho ones.

Since dogs pick up on their owner's emotions, one way to calm your dog is to calm yourself.

West Highland white terrier

Mixed breed

YOU SCARE ME. MAKE ONE MORE MOVE, AND I'LL ATTACK.

Bordeaux mastiff

CHECK OUT THE CANINES!

THIS PROFESSIONAL dog trainer shows a video pointing out the warning signs of a dog ready to bite.

FROM YOUTUBE:
http://tinyurl.com/howtospeakdogthreatened

AGGRESSIVE

Cute terriers were bred to catch rats. Because of that, they can snap and bite. Huge Newfoundlands, designed to pull carts and haul heavy fishnets, almost never snarl or snap. Selective breeding can also result in some dogs fighting more than others. These are all inherited traits. They depend on a dog's genes.

Genes are bits of biological information attached to DNA, which lies buried inside the cells of all living things. When breeders mix and match dogs to get the puppies they want, genes get rearranged. Breeders have tinkered so much by now that dogs have morphed into hundreds of types. Flip just one gene and what do you get? A Rottweiler instead of a dachshund. But you also end up tweaking the dog's behaviour.

Genetics isn't the whole story, however. A harsh upbringing can turn any dog vicious, and humane (positive) training can greatly improve behaviour.

An aggressive dog is a confident dog ready to prove it. Beware of a hard stare, forward ears, curled lip, and bared teeth. When combined with stiff legs; a high, stiff tail; and a snarl or growl, this dog is bad news. Whatever you do, don't run. He might chase you. Try to act submissive instead. Lower your eyes, blink, and force a yawn if you can. Keep your arms still and back slowly away.

President Theodore Roosevelt's bull terrier, Pete, chased the French ambassador through the White House and ripped out the seat of his trousers.

GO AWAY,
OR I'LL MAKE
YOU LEAVE.

CHECK OUT THE
CANINES!

THIS ROTTWEILER has found a new stuffed alligator friend, and shows his chops to protect it.

FROM YOUTUBE:
http://tinyurl.com/howtospeakdogaggressive

German shepherd

Chocolate Labrador retriever

SHAMED AND SUBMISSIVE

Uh-oh! You walk in the door and find your remote control chewed up on the floor. "Millie! How could you?" you scream, throwing your hands in the air. "Bad dog! Bad, bad dog." Millie hangs her head and slinks away, dragging her tail. *She knows what she did,* you think. *She should feel guilty.*

Trouble is, she really doesn't understand. All she knows is that there's a mess on the floor, and you're mad. She flattens her ears, shuts her mouth, and crouches down low to try to look small and helpless. If you're really angry, she'll lie flat on her back with her tail between her legs and whimper. These are signs of submission, not guilt. Your dog hopes that if she acknowledges you as the boss, you won't be angry anymore. What happened is this. Those little grooves surrounding the remote's buttons were full of dead skin cells that rubbed off your hands. So the remote smelled like you. To your lonesome dog, it was irresistible. Just replace the remote and buy her some exciting new chew toys. That will make you both happy. And maybe move the new remote somewhere she can't reach it!

CHECK OUT THE CANINES!

DENVER THE LAB lowers her eyes and shows her teeth in submissive gestures after her owner discovers she got into the kitty treats!

FROM YOUTUBE:
http://tinyurl.com/howtospeakdogshamed

Sam the golden retriever swallowed his owner's mobile phone. Following surgery to remove that, the mischievous canine ate a pair of her trousers!

GlobalPetFinder is a  system for pets. Worn on your dog's collar, it tracks his whereabouts and then notifies you by email or text.

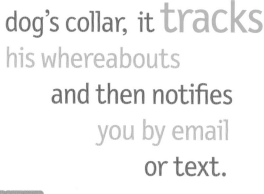
English pointer

CURIOUS AND EXCITED

A curious dog looks a lot like an alert dog, except his body is looser. Although he could be standing on tiptoe, his muscles are usually more relaxed. Again, his ears will be up and, maybe, slightly forward. His tail will also be up and swishing. The big thing to notice is his head. Curious dogs tilt their head from side to side.

You've heard the saying, "Curiosity killed the cat." Well, substitute "dog" for "cat". A German shepherd near Los Angeles, California, U.S.A., poked his head through a hole in a cement wall. Then he couldn't get it out! Luckily, a neighbour spotted his predicament and called Animal Services. Two officers rescued the curious dog.

So, if your dog ever turns up missing, he could be trapped. Start searching right away, and look in weird places. Check your neighbourhood garages, abandoned buildings, and local parks. Keep calling your dog's name as you search, and listen for an answering whimper. If your dog has a canine buddy, take him along. He may notice something you don't.

THIS IS ALL VEEEERY INTERESTING.

DR. GARY'S VET TIPS

BE SURE to get your dog microchipped, and keep both the chip and your dog's collar tags updated and registered. Then, if your hound gets lost, check with your local vets. Many dogs get returned because of that chip.

WHAT IS THIS DoG SAYING?

The Scenario

Meet Nubs, a dog living a tough life near a military post in Iraq. He befriended Major Brian Dennis, a pilot in the United States Marine Corp, who played with Nubs and rubbed his belly. One day, Dennis discovered Nubs was badly wounded. He cared for Nubs's injury, fed him, and slept by his side—treatment this poor dog had never known before. Nubs recovered, but Dennis's group was reassigned and pets weren't allowed, so his newfound buddy was left behind. Not for long, though!

Nubs took off after the convoy, crossed 75 miles (121 km) of blistering desert sand, and found his marine! There was no separating the two after that, and Nubs eventually headed back to the United States to live with Dennis and his family.

You Be the Expert

What makes a dog like Nubs happy? Are all dogs good or are there "bad" dogs that are just unhappy and miserable? And who's responsible for making our dogs happy?

All dogs can potentially be happy. Most important to them is love and having their needs met. Nubs was a dog desperate for love and care, and once he received it, he wasn't about to let go. Some people shower their pooches with things. They buy them four-poster beds, suede jackets, and diamond-studded collars. Is that what dogs need? Of course not. Proud-hearted Nubs just craved love and human companionship. Your dog does, too.

A dog's physical needs are simple—and cheap. Give your pet food, clean drinking water, and a warm, safe place to sleep. Groom his coat, take him to the veterinarian for regular checkups, and bathe him when he's dirty.

Building Your Bond

Meeting a dog's emotional needs is harder, because that takes time. Training and playing with your pooch is what makes you close. A well-mannered dog who obeys basic commands is easy to take places, and going anywhere together enriches your dog's life and sharpens his mind. Sharing new experiences goes a long way toward building your relationship.

Playing together helps, too. One of Dr. Gary's favourite playthings is a ChuckIt. This lets dog owners toss a ball much further than normal. Using it, you can throw a tennis ball fast and far for your dog to retrieve.

The bond between Major Dennis and Nubs is heartwarming. But it's not unique. Follow our advice, and your pooch will become equally devoted. He'll think of you as his person, and he'll never let you go!

UNDERSTANDING PET-IQUETTE

Minding your manners around dogs

 Avoid sending false signals. Dogs read every move we make. So if you always grab your jacket before taking Lucy out, try not to do that around her unless she can go, too.

 Crouch down and keep your hands low when saying "hi" to a new dog. If you stand and bend over to stroke him, you're acting like the top dog. No wonder some dogs take offence.

 Look dogs in the ear, not in their eyes. Dogs consider staring rude and take it as a challenge.

 Try to control your tone of voice. Always being yelled at or crossly spoken to makes dogs unhappy. They don't need to understand the words. They recognize the tone.

 Do your best to stay calm. Dogs pick up our emotions. So if you're nervous, your dog will know it and get nervous, too.

Shepherd-rottweiler mix

MEET AND GREET

SAYING "HI" TO A NEW DoG

1 Always ask the dog's owner for permission before trying to make friends. If the owner says it's okay, start by standing still and observing. Is the dog panting, licking, yawning, shivering, or raising one paw? Has he lowered his tail or pulled back his ears? Remember, those are signs of stress. If any are present, back off and let the dog relax.

2 Like us, dogs can change moods in an instant. So even if the dog acts calm, don't approach him head-on or stare directly into his eyes. Those things scare dogs. Turn your body sideways so that you look less threatening. Avert your eyes. Don't wave your arms or make any sudden movements. Keep your body quiet, speak softly, and wait. Let the dog come to you.

3 If he does, stand still and let him sniff you. Keep your hands to yourself, and don't pull anything—tail or ears. If the dog stays close, scratch him under his chin and tell him what a good dog he is. See if the dog moves closer to you.

4 Is the dog's body loose and wiggly? Are his eyes, ears, and mouth relaxed? If yes, try stroking his back or side. Use long, slow strokes, and don't stroke him on the head or lean over him. Then wait again. If the dog asks for more, congratulations! You've made a new friend.

Shepherd-collie mix

Beagle

PEOPLE ♥ DOGS

AN AGES-OLD LOVE AFFAIR

> Early humans, in what is now Israel, place two bodies—a woman and a dog—in the same grave. This is the earliest fossil evidence of human beings loving and living with a canine companion.

> Fifty dogs guard the Greek city of Corinth, while the people sleep. Suddenly enemy soldiers attack. They kill every dog but one. Soter, the sole survivor, races to the city gates and barks an alarm. The city is saved.

ABOUT 10,000 B.C.	2600 TO 2100 B.C.	A.D. 23–79

> Ancient Egyptians paint murals and inscribe collars with the names of some of their favourite dogs— Brave One, Antelope, Reliable, North-wind, and even (jokingly, we hope!) Useless.

> In Ethiopia, Africa, the Tonobari and Ptoenphae peoples select a dog as their king. The dog-king wears a crown and lives in a palace. Wagging his tail means he's pleased. A growl can condemn a man.

> Pilgrims bring two dogs with them to the New World, a big mastiff and a lively English springer spaniel. Who do they see when they first arrive? Six Indians walking a dog!

> Barry the St. Bernard lives in a monastery high in the Swiss Alps. This hero dog single-pawedly saves the lives of more than 40 people who get lost or trapped in the snow-covered mountain pass.

1620　　　**1800–1812**　　　**ABOUT 1865**

> Peps the Cavalier King Charles spaniel helps German composer Richard Wagner write his famous opera, *The Valkyrie*. As Wagner sings and plays, Peps listens. The parts he likes stay in. The parts he doesn't get tossed.

> Aibo, the world's first robot dog, goes on sale. Programmed to move by itself, the £1600 pretend pet recognizes its owner's face and obeys 100 commands. It even shows anger by turning its eyes red.

> Lassie the collie moves from being the hero of a popular book called *Lassie Come Home* to the star of a long-running American television series. Strangely enough, even though "Lassie" is another word for "girl", only boy dogs have ever played that role.

> Rin Tin Tin, the German shepherd rescued from a World War I battlefield, becomes the first canine movie star. He makes 27 movies and earns millions. When he dies, every newspaper in America prints his obituary.

1922   **1939**   **1954**   **1999**

> Toto, in the movie *The Wizard of Oz*, is played by a female cairn terrier named Terry, who was abandoned by her owners. They took Terry to a professional dog trainer to be housebroken and never came back for her. The trainer recognized Terry's talent and put her in movies.

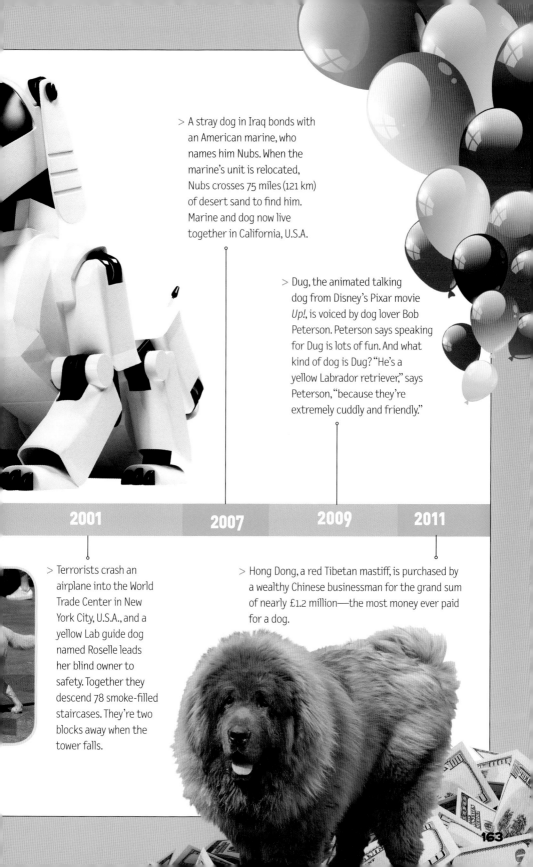

> A stray dog in Iraq bonds with an American marine, who names him Nubs. When the marine's unit is relocated, Nubs crosses 75 miles (121 km) of desert sand to find him. Marine and dog now live together in California, U.S.A.

> Dug, the animated talking dog from Disney's Pixar movie *Up!*, is voiced by dog lover Bob Peterson. Peterson says speaking for Dug is lots of fun. And what kind of dog is Dug? "He's a yellow Labrador retriever," says Peterson, "because they're extremely cuddly and friendly."

2001 **2007** **2009** **2011**

> Terrorists crash an airplane into the World Trade Center in New York City, U.S.A., and a yellow Lab guide dog named Roselle leads her blind owner to safety. Together they descend 78 smoke-filled staircases. They're two blocks away when the tower falls.

> Hong Dong, a red Tibetan mastiff, is purchased by a wealthy Chinese businessman for the grand sum of nearly £1.2 million—the most money ever paid for a dog.

BIG & LITTLE DoGS

(EVEN DOGS THAT HAVE NO HAIR!)

From Great Dane to Yorkshire terrier, today's domestic dog comes in hundreds of shapes and sizes. For centuries, people have mixed and matched dogs to get whatever they wanted—or needed. Almost every breed has come about because somebody, somewhere, needed a dog to help them do their job. Even today, when some dogs are being bred just for looks, most dogs enjoy having work to do. Check out some of these popular and fascinating dog breeds!

POMERANIAN

HOMELAND Iceland and Lapland

IDENTIFYING FEATURES Tiny, compact body weighing four to five pounds (1.8–2.3 kg), bright eyes, and a fluffy coat

ORIGINAL JOB Herding sheep (This was before "Poms" were bred to be so small.)

FUN TO KNOW Poms are a celebrity favourite. Singer Britney Spears, actress Hilary Duff, and basketball player Kobe Bryant all own Pomeranians. An adorable-looking Pom named Boo may be the world's most popular dog. He has nearly six million "likes" on his Facebook page.

LABRADOR RETRIEVER

HOMELAND Newfoundland, Canada

IDENTIFYING FEATURES A drip-dry coat, webbed feet, and a thick, otter tail

ORIGINAL JOB Jumping off boats to retrieve fishing nets in the Labrador Sea, which is how they got their name

FUN TO KNOW For 22 straight years, calm, dependable black Labs, yellow Labs, and chocolate Labs have been named America's most popular breed. Quick-learning Labs make wonderful pets and devoted service dogs. They guide the blind, assist hearing-impaired people, and help with search and rescue.

Golden retriever

Beagle

BEAGLE

HOMELAND Unknown, but most likely England

IDENTIFYING FEATURES Small and muscular, with soft brown eyes, floppy ears, a smooth coat, and a white tip on its tail

ORIGINAL JOB Hunting rabbits and hares

FUN TO KNOW Compulsive sniffers, beagles follow their nose. They like working in a pack. Hunters bred into them their white-tipped tail, so they could easily spot them running ahead. Snoopy, a character in the comic strip 'Peanuts' is probably the most famous fictitious Beagle.

CAVALIER KING CHARLES SPANIEL

HOMELAND England

IDENTIFYING FEATURES 13–18 pounds (6–8 kg); silky coat; long, feathered ears; and large, soft, brown eyes

ORIGINAL JOB Companion dog

FUN TO KNOW Named after King Charles II, of Great Britain, these ultimate lapdogs want nothing more than to be with people. King Charles found them so comforting that he passed a royal decree allowing the dogs inside any public place in England. This includes the Houses of Parliament. The law still stands!

DALMATIAN

HOMELAND Researchers don't agree, but possibly Egypt

IDENTIFYING FEATURES Recognized by their black or brown spots on a white coat

ORIGINAL JOB Known as coach dogs, they ran alongside and cleared the way for horse-drawn carriages and fire wagons.

FUN TO KNOW Dalmatian puppies are born white. The spots appear as they get older. Adult dogs are spotted all over, with polka-dotted bellies and spots inside their mouths. Each dog's spot pattern is as unique as a zebra's stripes.

Golden retriever

CHINESE CRESTED TERRIER

HOMELAND Unknown, but more likely Mexico than China

IDENTIFYING FEATURES Bare-naked, except for tufts of fur on head and feet

ORIGINAL JOB Rat hunting on Chinese sailing ships

FUN TO KNOW You've heard the saying, "She's so ugly that she's cute." Well, that holds true for Chinese crested terriers. These gentle family dogs come in two varieties—powderpuff and hairless. Hairless types have won six of the last ten "Ugliest Dog" contests!

DACHSHUND

HOMELAND Germany

IDENTIFYING FEATURES Stubby legs and a body so long that people joke he looks like a sausage!

ORIGINAL JOB Crawling into deep, underground tunnels to hunt badgers

FUN TO KNOW Popular in Germany since the 1500s, dachshunds didn't become a favourite in the United States until the early 1930s. At that time, many Americans began living in small city apartments. They liked the sausage-shaped dogs because they fit easily under their furniture!

GERMAN SHEPHERD

HOMELAND Germany

IDENTIFYING FEATURES Longer than they are tall, with bushy tails and erect ears, these dogs look very wolf-like.

ORIGINAL JOB Bred by a German army captain to help soldiers on the battlefield

FUN TO KNOW German shepherds are among the top ten most popular dogs in the UK. Many German shepherd puppies' ears don't stand erect until after they have finished teething. For a while, some pups even have one ear up and the other ear down!

POODLE

HOMELAND Countries in northern Europe

IDENTIFYING FEATURES Very curly coat, often paired with haircuts that leave part of their body bald and part covered with pom-poms

ORIGINAL JOB A water dog for retrieving ducks

FUN TO KNOW Supremely intelligent, and a family favourite, poodles love to learn and perform. Between 1999 and 2003, a toy poodle named Chanda-Leah held the Guinness World Record for the dog that knew the most tricks. She could perform more than 1,000 stunts!

YORKSHIRE TERRIER

HOMELAND
Northern England

IDENTIFYING FEATURES Blue and tan lapdog, with a long, silky coat that parts in the middle and sweeps the floor

ORIGINAL JOB Kept in England's cotton mills to chase rats

FUN TO KNOW Number six on America's most popular dog breed list, Yorkies often wear bows in their hair and look so adorable that ladies carry them around in their handbags. But those bows actually serve a purpose. They keep the pampered pooches' long locks away from their food and out of their eyes!

GOLDEN RETRIEVER

HOMELAND
Scotland

IDENTIFYING FEATURES Long-haired, yellow dogs with friendly eyes, webbed feet, and a heavily feathered tail

ORIGINAL JOB Retrieving ducks from the water

FUN TO KNOW Goldies are loyal. One named Baxter was tied out with his brother on a double lead, when both went missing. Two weeks passed. Then Baxter showed up. When his grateful owner went to get him, he led her into the woods and straight to his brother, whose lead was caught on some brush.

MIXED BREED

HOMELAND Could be anywhere

IDENTIFYING FEATURES Available in all sizes, shapes, colours, and patterns

ORIGINAL JOB Staying alive

FUN TO KNOW Most of the world's dogs are mongrels. Mongrels are mixed-breed dogs that come about naturally, without any interference from humans. Mongrels make devoted pets. After getting lost, one marathoner mongrel named Bobby walked 2,550 miles (4,104 km) from Indiana to Oregon, U.S.A., to find his family.

Bearded collie mix

PuPPY
KEEPSAKES YOU CAN MAKE

PUPPY PRINTS

1. Go outside. This could get messy.

2. Pour some food colouring into the bowl.

3. Gently dry your dog's nose or wipe his paw with a paper towel.

4. Dip a clean paper towel into the food colouring and dab a good bit of colour onto your dog's nose. Keep him from licking it off for a few seconds by showing him a doggie treat.

5. Press the pad against the front of your dog's nose, letting it curve around the sides, so you pick up all the bumps and dips. You may have to try this more than once to get it right.

6. For a paw, dip the sponge brush into the food colouring, and paint it all over the bottom of one of your dog's front paws. Lay the pad of paper on the ground and press your dog's paw onto it. Use your other hand to dangle a treat in front of him.

7. Lay the pad on a work surface and let it dry completely.

8. Wipe off your dog's nose or paw and give him the treat.

9. Frame and hang your masterpiece. You can also add a photo of your dog and a lock of his fur for a cool keepsake.

WHAT YOU'LL NEED:

- **PAPER TOWELS** (for nose) or a **SPONGE BRUSH** (for paws)
- **FOOD COLOURING** in whatever colour you prefer
- **BOWL**
- **SMALL PAD** of paper
- **A WILLING** dog
- **DOGGIE TREATS**

A FUN way to honour your dog is to make a noseprint of his schnoz. Look closely at the pattern of bumps and dips on the bald tip of your dog's nose. This pattern plus the outline of his nostrils make up his noseprint. A dog's noseprint is as unique to him as your fingerprints are to you. You can do the same thing with your dog's paw.

WHAT YOU'LL NEED:

- **MIXING BOWL**
- **BAKING TRAY** and **COOKING OIL SPRAY**
- **PEANUT BUTTER**
- **CANNED BEEF** or **CHICKEN BROTH**
- **FLOUR**
- **ROLLED OATS**
- **CINNAMON**
- **APPLESAUCE AND/OR BANANAS**

THUMBPRINT TREATS

1. Preheat oven to 165 °C (Gas 3).

2. Lightly coat a baking tray with cooking oil spray.

3. Put in a bowl and stir:
   125 g creamy peanut butter
   250 ml canned beef or chicken broth

4. Microwave on high for one minute—just until mixture becomes a liquid.

5. Add to the bowl:
   250 g flour
   50 g rolled oats
   2 teaspoons cinnamon

6. Mix with a fork, until dough hangs together. Fill the sheet with balls of dough half as big as Ping-Pong balls, set about 5 cm apart. Use your thumb to press a well into each cookie. Bake at 165 °C (Gas 3) for 15 minutes. Turn the oven off and leave cookies in the oven until cool.

7. Store in refrigerator or freezer. Just before serving, fill the cookie wells with little dabs of apple-sauce or mashed banana. Makes about 30 treats.

English bulldog

PaWS, LOOK, & LiSTEN QUiZ

DOGS TALK ALL THE TIME. But it's up to us to pay attention. Take this quiz to discover how careful listening can keep you safe.

1. Kids are most often bitten by
- A. Big dogs.
- B. Strays.
- C. Pets belonging to family and friends.
- D. Pit bulls.

2. Dogs sometimes bite when they're
- A. Protecting their territory.
- B. Feeling afraid.
- C. Startled.
- D. All of the above.

3. If a strange dog runs toward you, you should:
- A. Turn sideways and stand still.
- B. Scream and run away.
- C. Shake a stick in his face.
- D. Throw a rock at him.

4. What makes a dog mean?
- A. Being teased.
- B. Being kicked.
- C. Being tied up all the time.
- D. All of the above.

Answers to Stay Safe Around Dogs

1. C. All dogs can bite, even a cuddly pug. That's why banning certain breeds doesn't work. And few kids get bitten by strays. Most times it's a neighbour's dog or the family pet.

2. D. People protect their property and lives. And some come up swinging if they're startled awake. Dogs do the same, only they might defend "their" pavement, too.

3. A. Sticks and stones anger dogs, and motion excites them to chase. Large dogs can bound along at 40 mph (64 kph). Even a Chihuahua can outrun you. So stop moving, and freeze in place.

4. D. Being bullied or tormented makes any animal angry. With dogs, being kept chained or forced to live alone outside also can do it. Dogs long to be with people.

5. When meeting a strange dog with his owner, you should

   A. Give him a hug.

   B. Pat him on the head.

   C. Let the dog come to you.

   D. Grab his paw and "shake".

6. Never disturb a dog that is

   A. Playing.

   B. Inside a parked car.

   C. Howling.

   D. Sniffing the ground.

7. What's your best defense if a dog attacks?

   A. Shove your rucksack into his mouth.

   B. Drop and curl into a ball.

   C. Cover your ears and face.

   D. All of the above.

8. What's the best sign that a dog is friendly?

   A. He's wagging his tail.

   B. His ears are back.

   C. He's showing some teeth.

   D. His whole body looks loose and wiggly.

Bordeaux mastiff

5. C. Dogs hate being grabbed and prefer taking the lead. Also, think of the last time somebody patted you on the head. Did it make you feel small? Dogs don't like it either.

6. B. A dog shut in a car feels trapped. It can't run away. Neither can a dog on a lead. Beware of dogs that are eating or caring for puppies, too. They might be in guarding mode.

7. D. Posties hide behind their mail-bags. But any object will help. If you're empty-handed, drop to the ground. Curl up and lock your hands behind your neck to protect your face. Then freeze.

8. D. Never judge a dog by one part alone. Ear, tail, mouth, and body positions all have multiple meanings. Always look at the whole dog.

ReSOURCES

Pros Who Can Help

Association of Pet Dog Trainers (APDT)

The Association of Pet Dog Trainers educates dog owners by helping them find training classes and one-to-one lessons for their dogs. APDT trainers undergo rigorous assessment to ensure they have the necessary skills to train your dog. Use the "Local Dog Trainers" tab to find trainers in your area.

» www.apdt.co.uk

Blue Cross for Pets

Blue Cross for Pets offers treatment and re-homing services for a variety of pets every year. They also provide education and workshops to promote the importance of being a responsible pet owner.

» www.bluecross.org.uk

Cruelty Free International

This international organization campaigns against experimenting on animals all over the world. It investigates and challenges organizations that use animal testing, and promotes alternative methods.

» www.crueltyfreeinternational.org

Dogs Trust

Dogs Trust is the largest dog welfare charity in the UK. Their website offers advice on caring for dogs and lots of information about adopting dogs from their re-homing centres.

» www.dogstrust.org.uk

Kennel Club

The Kennel Club oversees thousands of dog shows all over the UK and keeps a registry of pedigree dogs. Its site has info about breeds, contests, dog care, and fun activities.

» www.thekennelclub.org.uk

Royal Society for the Prevention of Cruelty to Animals (RSPCA)

This is the UK's largest animal welfare charity. Under the "Advice and Welfare" tab, you'll find great dog care tips. You can also click on "Ask a question" and ask experts at the RSPCA questions about dog welfare.

» www.rspca.org.uk

Scottish Society for the Prevention of Cruelty to Animals (Scottish SPCA)

The Scottish SPCA is Scotland's animal welfare charity—it has been helping animals in Scotland for over 175 years. They organize events, raising money to help educate children to look after their pets well, as well as helping re-home thousands of animals each year.

» www.scottishspca.org

Wood Green, The Animals Charity

Wood Green, The Animals Charity cares for and re-homes all types of animals. Under the "Pet advice" tab, there is plenty of information about how to care for canines—from how to train your dog to the importance of vaccinating your pet.

» www.woodgreen.org.uk

On Screen and In Print

BOOKS

A Dog's Guide to Humans
Karen Davison
CreateSpace, 2013

A Dog's Purpose
W. Bruce Cameron
Pan, 2017

101 Amazing Facts about Dogs
Jenny Kellett
CreateSpace, 2016

DOGS: A Kid's Book of Dog Breeds
Eve Heidi Bine-Stock
E & E Publishing, 2015

i-SPY Dogs
i-SPY
HarperCollins, 2016

**National Geographic Kids:
Everything Dogs**
Becky Baines
National Geographic Society, 2012

**National Geographic Kids 125 True
Stories of Amazing Animals**
National Geographic Kids Magazine
National Geographic Society, 2012

MOVIES

My Dog: An Unconditional Love Story
New Video, 2009

**Nature: Dogs That Changed the
World**
Questar, 2007

NOVA: Dogs and More Dogs
PBS, 2004

NOVA: Dogs Decoded
PBS, 2010

Through a Dog's Eyes
PBS, 2010

WEBSITES

National Geographic Kids
animals.nationalgeographic.com/animals/
mammals/domestic-dog
animals.nationalgeographic.com/animals/
mammals/wolf
kids.nationalgeographic.com/kids/photos/
dogs-with-jobs
kids.nationalgeographic.com/kids/photos/
gallery/dogs

Animal Planet
http://Animal.discovery.com/tv/dogs-101

A Kid's Guide to Dog Care
www.loveyourdog.com

INDeX

ILLUSTRATION CREDITS

Published by Collins
An imprint of HarperCollins Publishers
Westerhill Road
Bishopbriggs
Glasgow G64 2QT
www.harpercollins.co.uk

In association with National Geographic
Partners, LLC

NATIONAL GEOGRAPHIC and the Yellow Border
Design are trademarks of the National
Geographic Society, used under license.

First published 2013

ISBN 9780008257910

10 9 8 7 6 5 4 3 2 1

Printed in China

If you would like to comment on any aspect of
this book, please contact us at the above
address or online.
natgeokidsbooks.co.uk
collins.reference@harpercollins.co.uk

Paper from responsible sources.